What history is for

Essays in honour of Professor John Foster

"What history is for"

First published in 2024 by Manifesto Press

Manifesto Press
Ruskin House
23 Coombe Road
Croydon CR0 1BD

Typeset in Bodoni Std and Gill Sans MT pro
Designed by Nick Wright

ISBN 978-1-907464-69-0

press@manifestopress.coop
manifestopress.coop

Contents

Contributors

Gavin Brewis is a published PhD researcher and occasional lecturer at Glasgow Caledonian University. He is a member of the Scottish Poverty and Inequality Research Unit, an Associate Member of the Scottish Centre for Crime and Justice Research and sits on the Scottish Graduate School for Arts and Humanities' Doctoral Research Committee. His research focuses on class and culture, and psychosocial trauma and emotions.

Pauline Bryan is the convener of the Red Paper Collective and co-edited *Class, Nation and Socialism: The Red Paper on Scotland 2014*. She is currently working a book to mark the 50th anniversary of the first Red Paper on Scotland. She is a regular contributor to the *Morning Star* and was appointed a Labour Peer by Jeremy Corbyn in 2018.

Chik Collins studied social sciences at Paisley College of Technology (now UWS) in the mid-1980s. He later returned to undertake a PhD, supervised by John Foster, and then spent over two decades working there, becoming Professor of Applied Social Science. In 2019 he was made Rector of the University of the Faroe Islands and in 2023 became Director of the Glasgow Centre for Population Health.

Kenny Coyle is a writer, editor and publisher. He is the Director of Praxis Press. A regular contributor to the *Morning Star*, he is author of several Communist Party pamphlets on Marxism, as well as international politics. He has lived and worked in various parts of Asia since 2000. Kenny has also collaborated with John Foster on several projects over the years.

James Crossley is Professor of Religion and Politics at MF Oslo and the Director of the Centre for the Critical Study of Apocalyptic and Millenarian Movements. He is author of *Spectres of John Ball: The Peasants' Revolt in English Political History, 1381-2020* (2022) and a forthcoming biography of A.L. Morton.

Mary Davis is Visiting Professor of Labour History at Royal Holloway, University of London. She has, from a Marxist perspective, written, broadcast and lectured widely on women's history, labour history, imperialism and racism. She currently serves on the *Morning Star* Management Committee, the Sylvia Pankhurst Memorial Committee and is Secretary of Marx Memorial Library and Workers' School.

Susan Galloway is a member of the Communist Party's Govan Branch and a former Scottish Secretary of the Party. She has worked in research roles in the children's sector, local government, higher education and the trade union movement for over thirty-five years.

Robert Griffiths is the General Secretary of the Communist Party of Britain. His books include *S.O. Davies–A Socialist Faith* (1983); *Streic! Streic! Streic!* (1986); *Driven by Ideals: A History of ASLEF* (2005); *Killing No Murder–South Wales and the Great Railway Strike of 1911* (2009); *Granite and Honey: The Story of Phil Piratin, Communist MP* (2012 with Kevin Marsh); *Marx's Das Kapital and Capitalism Today* (2018); and *Reddest of the Reds: S.O. Davies, MP and Miners' Leader* (2019).

David Horsley was a primary school teacher in Lambeth, South London and Ewarton, Jamaica for over 30 years. Radicalised by anti-colonial struggles of the 1960s, he serves on the Communist Party's Anti-Racist Anti-Fascist Commission. The focus of his research is on revealing the contributions of Black Communists in Britain. He is the author of *The Political Life and Times of Claudia Jones* and *Billy Strachan, 1921-1998*.

Marjorie Mayo is vice-chair of the Marx Memorial Library and Workers' School trustees and editor of *Theory & Struggle*. She is Emeritus Professor of Community Development at Goldsmiths, University of London. She has researched and written widely on community education and development, and community cohesion and solidarity.

Vijay Prashad is an Indian historian, journalist and author of forty books. He is Executive Director of Tricontinental: Institute for Social Research and Chief Correspondent for *Globetrotter*. He is also the Chief Editor of LeftWord Books (New Delhi) and a senior non-resident fellow at Chongyang Institute for Financial Studies, Renmin University of China.

Roger Seifert read PPE at Oxford University. He received an MBA from the London Business School and his PhD from the London School of Economics. He worked for the Incomes Data Service before becoming Professor of Industrial Relations at Keele University (1992-2008) and then Wolverhampton University (2008-2018). He specialises in trade unions, strikes, public sector pay, labour history, and the role of the state in industrial relations.

Jonathan White is the author of *Making Our Own History: A User's Guide to Marx's Historical Materialism* (2021). He is also assistant editor of *Theory & Struggle* and as well as *Communist Review*, and a trustee of the Marx Memorial Library and Workers' School.

Editors

Elaine McFarland is Emeritus Professor of History at Glasgow Caledonian University. Her research interests include Irish Protestant migration to Scotland and the military history of the Great War. She is currently editor of the *Scottish Historical Review* Monograph series.

Jim Whiston recently retired as the director of the housing association, Ayrshire Housing. He is a member of the Communist Party's Housing and Progressive Federalism Commissions

Images

Front Cover: Tony Conway
John Foster: Vaughan Melzer

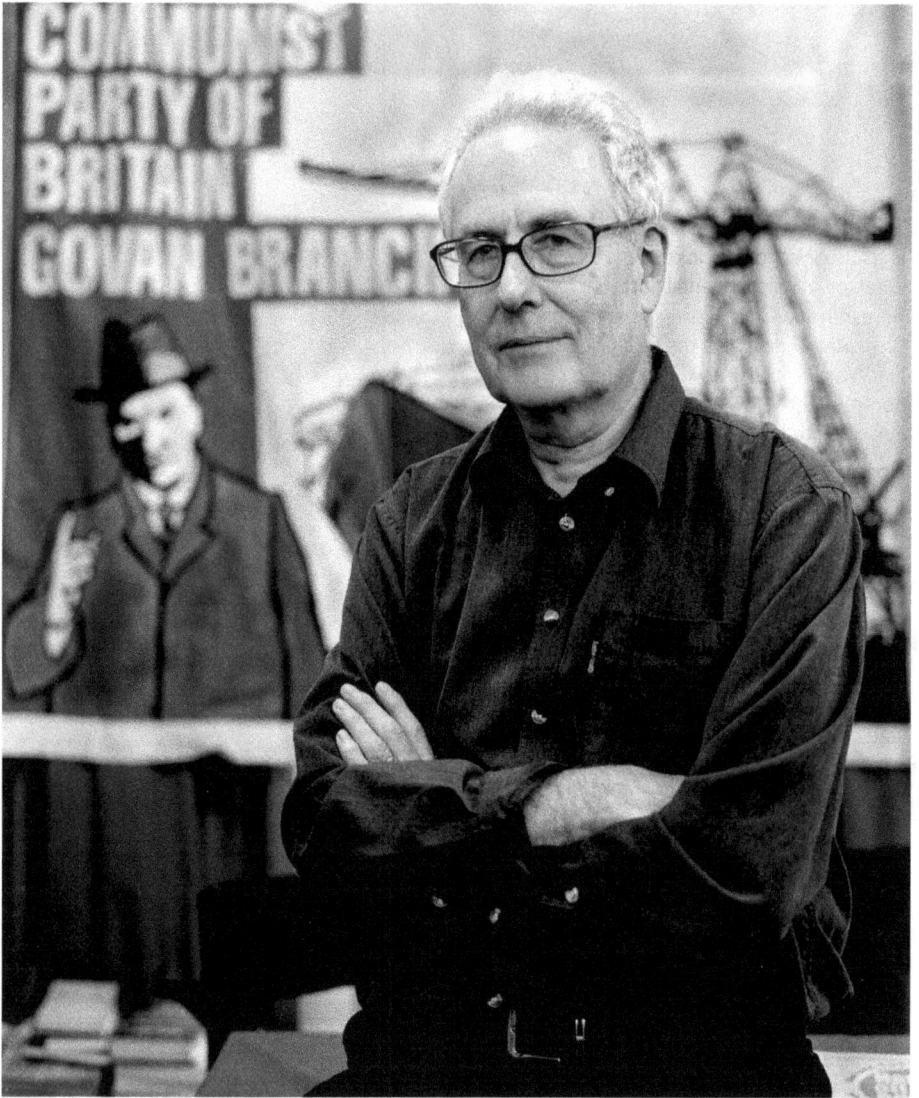

Elaine McFarland and Jim Whiston

Foreword

THIS HAS BEEN a very easy book to edit. John Foster has made a major contribution to Marxist historiography and political economy for well over 50 years. In doing so, he has carried forward the work of Britain's politically committed Marxist historians from the 1930s onwards. Like them, his work is written with a practical purpose whether it is accessible historical studies or pamphlets engaging with the issues of today for the labour and progressive movements, both at home and internationally. Yet, perhaps even more important is the personal impact that he has made on a generation of academics, activists and students, who are represented among the collection's contributors.

The essays and the accompanying bibliography reflect the huge range of his work. Some of these are retrospective reflections on the major themes of his writing, while others analyse its current practical application in raising political understanding around the national question, state power and imperialism. They also include new work from researchers who have benefited from John's influence.

Above all, this has been a collaborative project. We would firstly like to thank the contributors who have honoured John with their essays. Further thanks are due to Chik Collins, Keith Stoddart and Eben Williams who helped ensure the bibliography's completeness. We are also grateful to Paul Macgee and Nick Wright at Manifesto Press for producing such an attractive volume. Vaughan Melzer kindly allowed the use of her engaging portraits of John on the frontspiece and back cover. As John is known to all for his endearing modesty, we would finally like to acknowledge his forbearance when this project was first suggested.

ROBERT GRIFFITHS

Introduction

MARX AND ENGELS had much to say about history and historiography. They researched, assessed and reproduced the work of chroniclers and historians, from ancient Greece and Rome to early medieval Wales and bourgeois France and England, on an epic scale. The fifty volumes of their *Collected Works* are peppered with judgements about individual historians, always taking account of the impact of society on their attitudes and work.

The founders of the Marxist world outlook understood the limitations and distortions that could arise in the recording and retelling of history; how economic, social and political conditions can dictate, disorientate and corrupt those activities; and how an historian's remoteness from contemporary realities can also limit and distort their understanding, analysis and conclusions concerning the past.

This is not to offer a Marxist variant of Henry Ford's assertion that 'History is bunk'. Marx and Engels fully recognised the value of uncovering, and understanding the past, learning lessons from it and applying these as appropriate to the struggle to create a better tomorrow. They held numerous ancient scribes and modern historians (Edward Spencer Beesly, Francois Mignet) in high regard, while excoriating the exertions of others whose prime intention was to serve the interests of the ruling class and themselves (Lord John Russell, Mikhail Pogodin, Adolphe Thiers).

This approach made Marx and Engels formidable historians in their own right, not least because they were also activists in real-time movements for resistance, reform and revolution. Of course, as they themselves would happily have anticipated, their accounts of significant periods and events in history have been enriched and even corrected by subsequent studies.

The result of all this is that they have provided us today with a model of the ideal historian: one who deals in material reality, in the conditions and relations of its production and reproduction; who concentrates on the decisive factors and forces of history, not on the trivial and superficial; who fearlessly seeks the truth from verifiable facts; who understands and applies the dialectical method; who has no delusion or pretence of neutrality or of an elevated, impartial objectivity, above the realities of class society and class struggle; an historian who seeks not only to understand society but to change it.

Which brings me to John Foster, social historian and political revolutionary. He follows not only in the footsteps of Marx and Engels; he strides into unexplored or at least under-explored territories. And in doing so, he has exhibited all the qualities that his ideological mentors failed to find in their bourgeois and petty-bourgeois contemporaries.

John made his reputation with a ground-breaking study of unfolding social and industrial relations in Oldham, South Shields and Northampton: *Class Struggle and the Industrial Revolution: Early Industrial Capitalism in Three English Towns*.[1] Such eminent historians as Eric Hobsbawm and E.P. Thompson recognised the arrival of a brilliant new intellect at Harvey Kaye's school of The British Marxist Historians.[2]

Like his celebrated predecessors, John seeks the truth of what happened and why from the facts, meticulously researched, clearly presented, surgically examined and skilfully interpreted.

As a dedicated Communist Party member, he combined full-time employment in academia with full-time organising and campaigning in the Govan district of Glasgow, emerging as a tenants' leader who challenged landlords, developers, local councillors and later the Scottish Parliament in the interest of his working-class community.

Collaborating with Charles Woolfson, he recorded for posterity the inspirational, Communist-led work-in to save the Upper Clyde Shipbuilders and thousands of local jobs. In three books with Woolfson and other joint authors he has explored class struggle in Scotland's offshore oil industry.

Most recently, he has produced *Languages of Class Struggle: Communication and Mass Mobilisation in Britain and Ireland 1842-1972* and authored and co-authored two volumes of the history of the Transport & General Workers Union and Unite.[3]

In best dialectical fashion, John's intellectual and practical activities have penetrated and enriched each other. This has been particularly evident in his approach to two of the most important controversies of recent years: the national question in Scotland and Britain; and UK membership of the European Union.

In both cases, as secretary of the Communist Party's Scottish Committee and as international secretary of the Communist Party of Britain, John Foster utilised his profound grasp of Marxism, his knowledge of history and the lessons of practical experience to analyse these questions. Rooted in class politics, his materialist perspectives (for 'progressive federalism' and 'popular sovereignty' outside monopoly capital's EU) did not accord with the idealist, petty-bourgeois notions of many Scottish nationalists, nor those of an anti-working class section of the *Guardian*-reading intelligentsia.

His emphasis on building broad, progressive and non-sectarian alliances on every front and at every level on these and other issues has helped secure advances and victories ... and won him many allies, friends and admirers.

It has been my personal privilege – and an invaluable part of my own political education – to have worked closely with John for more than three decades in the leadership of the Communist Party. I have seen at close quarters the efficiency, judgement and integrity with which he has confronted challenges facing the party, the working class and humanity.

His momentous contribution to historiography and the struggle for peace, social progress and the cause of human self-liberation is perhaps best distilled in this resolution tabled by Labour and SNP members of the Scottish Parliament (MSPs):

80 Years of Commitment to Education, Activism and Socialism

The Parliament notes that 21 October 2020 is the 80th birthday of Professor John Foster; recognises the enormous contribution to learning that Professor Foster has made over his long academic career in Scotland from its beginning at University of Strathclyde to its conclusion at University of Paisley, now the University of the West of Scotland; compliments his unwavering commitment to both formal and informal education; commends his contribution to economics and history and, in particular, his writings on the Scottish Labour and trade union movement; notes his grassroots political activism within the Communist Party and unwavering commitment to the *Morning Star* newspaper and his community work that brought about significant advances in Govan, where he lived, and elsewhere across Scotland, in developing the tenants' movement, and celebrates his major influence on the wider political landscape of Scotland, including the re-establishment of the Scottish Parliament.

Given such an extraordinary tribute, it is all the more important that this volume of essays succeeds in doing justice to the life and work of an outstanding Marxist scholar.

Many contributions provide fresh insights into his achievements as a political thinker, activist and historian. Others raise questions and propose valuable perspectives on Black communist history and England's so-called Peasants' Revolt of 1381. Indeed, a world of challenges and crises is explored here, from exploitation and development in the Global South to urban violence and health in Scotland and Britain. Above all, this book is an historical, political and ideological celebration of the creative labours of Professor John Foster.

Notes

1   J. Foster, *Class Struggle and the Industrial Revolution: Early Industrial Capitalism in Three English Towns* (Weidenfeld and Nicolson, London: 1974).

2   H. J. Kaye, *The British Marxist Historians an Introductory Analysis* (Polity Press, Cambridge: 1984), 142-3.

3   *Languages of Class Struggle: Communication and Mass Mobilisation in Britain and Ireland 1842-1972* (Praxis Press, Glasgow: 2024); (With M. Davis), *UNITE History Volume 1 (1880-1931): The Transport and General Workers' Union (TGWU): Representing a Mass Trade Union Movement* (Liverpool University Press, Liverpool: 2022); *UNITE History Volume 4 (1960-1974): The Transport and General Workers' Union (TGWU): The Great Tradition of Independent Working Class Power* (Liverpool University Press, Liverpool: 2023).

1 MARY DAVIS

Historiography, class formation and class struggle

JOHN FOSTER'S lifetime of political engagement and scholarship has resulted in a vast corpus of published work which might at first glance appear eclectic in that it does not fit neatly into a single academic discipline. This prompts an inquiry as to whether there is a central leitmotif underlying the range and extent of his writings.

Of course, as a communist, all his work is either directly to inform the labour movement (for example, his many pamphlets published by the Communist Party), or is written from a socialist perspective. However, what unites all of them is Marxist theory. This equally applies to his academic work as a historian. But in this we see something much more fundamental – the practical application of Marx's theory of history and analytical method: historical materialism. There are very few historians alive today who have consistently and successfully embedded historical materialism as a foundational framework for their published work. John Foster is one of them. This historiographical chapter seeks to explore how his writings as a labour historian and also as a Marxist educator exemplifies this claim.

Foster's first published book, *Class Struggle and the Industrial Revolution* (1974) is an outstanding example of the application of Marx's method and Marxist theory to a detailed analysis of class formation and class struggle in England in the first half of the nineteenth century. Eric Hobsbawm's fulsome praise in his preface to the book notes its originality and the depth of its scholarship. But, in addition to the book's academic rigour, its most important feature is the purpose to which its scholarship is applied. The central tenet of the book is to analyse and illuminate the nature of the change which English capitalism underwent by the middle of the nineteenth century. This change, sometimes mistakenly defined as 'liberalisation', was one in which the working-class militancy evident in the first half of the nineteenth century, was effectively diluted by the emergence of a labour aristocracy which fractured class unity thereby weakening class struggle. In other words, by mid-century, for the ruling class, the threat to the stability of capitalist relations of production was averted, economic equipoise was restored, enabling Britain, as the first industrial nation, to become the 'workshop of the world'.

Noting this pivotal change is one thing, explaining it is much more difficult – this is the substance of the book. Foster notes that there have been negligible attempts at analysing why this change should have occurred when it did – or even whether or why it should have occurred at all. This lacuna is even truer today as it was when the book was written in 1974. Labour history as an academic discipline barely exists now. There has been a steady decline of interest in the subject of class from the supposedly influential 'golden age' of the labour movement in the 1940s and 1950s to its alleged decline in the 1980s and beyond. This decline has led to a historicist questioning of the role of working-class agency and class in general. Such turning away from the concept of class has had an inevitable impact on the interest in writing working-class history and organisation.

Nonetheless, for today's socialists an analysis of capitalist development and the nature of the asymmetrical struggle between capital and labour is vital not just for the understanding of labour and working-class history, but as a means of comprehending our own social reality from a Marxist perspective.

The originality of Foster's work lies in the fact that he sought to explain the historic decline in class consciousness in a unique way. He focussed his explanation on developments in three very different English towns in the first half of the nineteenth century. This was not a random choice – each of these towns, Oldham, Northampton and South Shields, displayed a distinct and different aspect of Britain's industrial development. Correspondingly, they also displayed different and distinct forms of working-class organisation and analogous expressions of class consciousness or, more narrowly in some cases, trade union consciousness. The contrast between the three towns and more particularly the contrast between Oldham, with a long-standing radical history and a burgeoning industrial capitalist economy based on the cotton industry, and the other two, serves to throw light on the book's two central questions. These questions are massive and form the substance of the study; namely, how industrial capitalism developed as a whole, and in this context how working-class consciousness developed, flourished, and subsequently declined. In this connection, Foster illuminates a central issue for Marxists today – how to understand what is commonly known as 'false consciousness', the obverse of class consciousness (in fact, his doctoral thesis was focussed on working-class consciousness). Although false consciousness undoubtedly serves a prop to aid capitalist domination, Foster argues that it cannot be seen simply as a product of bourgeois manipulation imposed from outside. He argues that it must be understood as a historical formation, one that undergoes change, and that such change is based upon a 'historically determined pattern of consumption.'[1] There is a dialectical relationship between the forces that seek to maintain traditional identity and those that attempt to challenge it. Or, as Marx put it, 'consciousness must be judged from the contradictions of material life.'[2]

So, this book cannot be pigeonholed into a convenient urban or social history category. Neither can it be seen as a 'specialist' study. Nor, despite its pages of statistical information on marriage rates, church attendance, occupational structure of the bourgeoisie (and much else), does it degenerate into antiquarianism. Its scope and vision transcends such categorisation. It is a work which exemplifies historical materialism both in substance and method and, as such, points to an understanding of the interplay between the forces and relations of production underlying the capitalist mode of production then and now.

This book and subsequent articles, pamphlets, lectures and Marx Memorial Library courses reveal the concrete application of historical materialism of Foster's work. In his chapter on 'British Imperialism and the Labour Aristocracy', Foster extends his analysis of class and class formation to the later nineteenth century – the epoch of imperialism.[3] In third quarter of the century the profitability of Britain's staple industries had provided the material base for the division and disunity of the working class. The instrument, facilitated by the profitability of Britain's staple industries, was the emergence of a better paid sector – the labour aristocracy, a term used by Lenin (although not invented by him). This facilitated a very important ideological shift as well as a material shift within the working class which had important repercussions for the labour movement.

However, the last quarter of the nineteenth century saw a massive economic decline – an end to Britain's place as 'the workshop of the world'. So how was division maintained? Did the labour aristocracy continue? The short answer is that the massive empire which had already given Britain a huge lead, saved the day. The labour aristocracy remained, but as John Foster points out, it existed in an altered form and as means of control it differed from the previous period. In this new period, empire expansion was accompanied by the twin ideologies of social imperialism and racism, both of which infected trade union consciousness with negative political repercussions, particularly within the leadership of the labour movement.

This chapter cannot do justice to the vast corpus of John's historical writings, all of which be they, journal articles, books or pamphlets are exemplars of the historian's craft. His published work is broad ranging in scope. It covers aspects of Scottish and Irish history, British and Scottish labour history, nationalism, class and class struggle with particular emphasis on seminal episodes of class confrontation (as on Clydeside and in Belfast in 1919, the 1926 General Strike, and the UCS Work-in). Academic rigour is the hallmark of his work. Everything he has written displays a thorough attention to historical evidence – to primary and secondary sources. This research is not the randomly empiricist. It is informed by materialist hypotheses designed to throw light on often undiscovered areas of 'history from below'. This has led to original discoveries especially in the field of labour history which in turn has stimulated important re-interpretations of pivotal historical moments. An example of this is his recent work on the 1920

Councils of Action.[4] In this pamphlet John Foster proves that the threat of a general strike in 1920 in defence of Soviet Russia not only marked the first occasion in which the leadership of the British Labour movement threatened action against the British government, but more importantly forced the government to abandon its policy of declaring war on the young Bolshevik state. This interpretation challenges the accepted view that the government was not swayed by the threat of mass action and that it would have changed its interventionist policy anyway. Foster's meticulous study of MI5 and Home Office papers, as well as his insight into the balance of left and right forces in the leadership of the TUC, shows conclusively that the traditional interpretation, first promulgated by Lloyd George, and largely accepted by historians, is wrong.

All Foster's work is linked by the common thread of historical materialism, but this begs the question of the way in which he comprehends the kernel of Marx's historical method. He takes issue with those academic Marxists who either reject or misinterpret the real essence of historical materialism and offer instead their own inadequate theories of historical change. In several articles and book chapters, he offers his view of the meaning of historical materialism. But first he pays tribute to Marxist historians who preceded him, notably the collective contribution of the Communist Party's History Group. This group, active in the 1940s and 50s, made a huge contribution to a Marxist understanding of history and social and economic change. Inspired by the Marxist economist Maurice Dobb, the group nurtured the work of historians such as Victor Kiernan, Dona Torr, Eric Hobsbawm, A.L. Morton, Christopher Hill, Rodney Hilton, John Saville, E.P. Thompson, Dorothy Thompson and many others. They divided their work into four main historical periods – ancient, medieval, the sixteenth and seventeenth centuries, as well as nineteenth century history. The group wrote accessible history grounded in an analysis of the material circumstances which could either limit or enable social change. Although the group continued to meet after 1956, it lost many of its prominent members who left the Communist Party in the wake of the Soviet intervention in Hungary. However, in the 1960s and 70s some of these historians, notably Thompson, Saville and Hobsbawm defended historical materialism against a new crop of pseudo-Marxist detractors, in particular Louis Althusser and his followers.

In the same communist tradition, John Foster continued the defence of Marx's historical method, notably against the critical attack launched by Francis Fukuyama in his influential book, *The End of History and the Last Man* (1992). Fukuyama argues that the demise of alternative models to liberal democracy, notably fascism and communism, meant that history itself has endowed liberal democracy as the triumphant survivor. Thus, like Hegel, Fukuyama announces the arrival of the end of history. Whereas for Hegel, this 'end' was the triumph of the Prussian state, for Fukuyama, history's destination is the victory of bourgeois democracy. Apart from questioning the credentials of liberalism, Foster attacks the philosophically idealist foundations of a view of history, which, although dialectical in its acknowledgment of historical progression, sees its ultimate goal as the triumph of the reified 'Idea'.[5] The real problem, according to Foster, is Fukuyama's espousal of the Hegelian dialectic rather than Marx's materialist dialectic.

Similarly, Foster is sharply critical of those writers who, in the 1970s, in the name of 'academic rigour' sought to give Marx an academically respectable status.[6] He cites the influence of Althusserian Structuralism and Analytical Marxism expressed in the work of such writers as M. Foucault, E.O. Wright, G.A. Cohen and many others. All are linked by a rejection of dialectics in general and dialectical materialism in particular. As Foster puts it, 'For all of these approaches the assertion of logical precision comes first, history second and there is no scope for any dialectical encounter on the way'.[7]

In his defence of dialectical and historical materialism, Foster cites many eminent Marxists and Marxist historians. However, his own words provide a cogent and accessible defence of Marx's method and deserve to be quoted in full, especially because it is this that marks the cornerstone of his own work as a historian. He summarises four essential arguments in defence of the integrity of Marx's work:

Defending Marx's understanding of the base not as static but as an active dialectical process, the contradictory interaction *between* the means and relations of production, one which provides the context for understanding the flux of superstructural debate.

Defending Marx's Method – one which matches this understanding and requires an overall analysis of social processes to secure, ultimately, definitions that encompass 'a rich totality of many determinations and relations'.

Understanding the role of the working-class movement, as a *movement*, one that crystallises the stage and intensity of the contradictions of the capitalist system, which carries forward the practical knowledge of those contradictions but which works within circumstances not of its own creation.

Understanding, finally, history as process in which classes ultimately express and act out the key contradictions in human progress, a process that cannot be grasped by simply abstracting and labelling specific elements. They must be understood as part of this continuing process.[8]

Foster acknowledges that adopting Marx's method is difficult because it means challenging the existing canons of academic discourse. In particular it means rejecting the structural Marxists insistence on 'the external application of pre-defined concepts to discrete fragments of experience.'[9] Instead, historical understanding of any given period or moment can only be achieved by dissecting the dialectical interplay between the forces and relations of production. This is the basis of grasping the essence of the change and movement of social processes as a whole – in other words, the understanding of foundational changes in the mode of production.

Foster's ability to synthesise his method and practice as a Marxist historian in an intelligible manner devoid of academic obscurantism, has made him an exceptional educator. This has been and still is the hallmark of his work at the Marx Memorial Library and Workers' School (MML). John has been involved in the work of MML for over 40 years – variously as a Trustee of many years and as its Secretary. He is currently Secretary of MML's Education Committee. In this capacity John has been the main author of three popular distance learning courses – 'Introduction to Marxist Economics', 'Crisis, Capitalism and Imperialism' and 'Trade Unions, Class and Power'. He has worked with a team of tutors, most of whom are his former students, to develop these courses, all of which attract applicants from all over Britain and internationally. He is now actively developing the Workers' School so that it can become the leading centre of Marxist education in Britain. In addition, John has played a major role in the team of authors from MML who have written the six-volume history of Unite the Union.

In this way, John is following in the footsteps of the MML's brilliant Marxist educators — James Klugmann, Robin Page Arnot and Andrew Rothstein (for whom he has unbounded admiration). He dedicated his pamphlet on the 1920 Councils of Action to Page Arnot and has written fulsomely about the contribution of Rothstein. Rothstein was chair and later president of the MML from 1945 to 1985, a post he shared for some of this time with Maurice Dobb. Rothstein 'led the library through four decades of dramatic redevelopment.'[10] When Rothstein died in 1994, John Foster bade 'Farewell to a Man of History'. He praised Rothstein as a historian: 'there was nothing pettifogging or academic about his work. Passion for exactitude would be more correct. There should be no fog of romantic wish fulfilment. Political practice demands the truth.'[11] He admired and delineated three aspects of Rothstein's work: as a defender of historical materialism, as a defender of Marxist principles of political action and as a Marxist who understood the dialectics of internationalism. In all this John wrote of Rothstein's 'unshakeable devotion to principle, diamond-hard resolution in defending it, exceptional personal modesty born of desire to explain and persuade, not to browbeat, the embodiment of the finest qualities of a Marxist and a teacher.'

I quote John's fulsome tribute to Rothstein not just as a matter of historical accuracy, but because every aspect of the qualities he applauds can be applied equally and with justification to John Foster himself. His own personal modesty would reject such a claim, but nonetheless his peers would endorse the description of John Foster as embodying the finest qualities of a Marxist, a Marxist historian and a teacher.

Notes

1   J. Foster, *Class Struggle and the Industrial Revolution: Early Industrial Capitalism in Three English Towns* (Methuen, London: 1974), 5.
2   From K. Marx, *Contribution to the Critique of Political Economy,* quoted in J. Foster, 'The end of history and historical materialism: A defence of Marxist dialectics, in M. Davis and M. Mayo (eds), *Marxism and Struggle; Toward the Millennium*, (Praxis Press, London: 1998), 34.
3   J. Foster, 'British Imperialism and the Labour Aristocracy', in J. Skelley (ed.), *The General Strike 1926*, (Lawrence & Wishart, London: 1976), 3-57.
4   J. Foster, *The Councils of Action 1920 and the British Labour Movement's Defence of Soviet Russia* (Manifesto Press, Croydon: 2017).
5   Foster, 'The End of History', in Davis and Mayo, *Marxism and Struggle*, 20-54.
6   Foster 'On Marx's Method and the Study of History', *Theory & Struggle*, 116 (2015), 53-59.
7   Foster 'On Marx's Method', 55
8   J. Foster, 'History and Marx's Method', in M. Davis (ed.) *Marx 200: The Significance of Marxism in the 21st Century* (Praxis Press, London: 2019), 37.
9   'On Marx's Method', 59.
10 J. Foster, (with M. Davis and R. Seifert) 'Three Communist Educators: Robin Page Arnot, James Klugmann and Andrew Rothstein', *Theory & Struggle*, 121 (2020), 108-125.
11 *Marx Memorial Library Bulletin*, 126 (1996), 14.

2 CHIK COLLINS

The political economy of population health in contemporary Scotland

IN SEPTEMBER 1983, I embarked on a programme in social science at Paisley College of Technology, where Professor John Foster was the youthful Head of the Department of Sociology and Politics.[1] Foster's year-long course in Historical Studies was a foundational part of the programme.

Six months later, the 1984-85 Miners' Strike was getting under way. I found myself by that stage equipped to write essays on everything from the Peasants' Revolt of the late fourteenth century, to Chartism, to the creation of the Keynesian Welfare State. However, more importantly, I was now able to understand what was happening, and what was at stake, in the colossal class struggle that was then getting underway. That understanding was almost entirely due to that Historical Studies course.

This encapsulates something essential about Foster's work. Foster does not seek for his work to be 'admired'. He seeks for it to be used to frame our understanding of, and engagement with, the issues and the struggles of the present and, through that, to contribute more effectively to the active creation of the future – a democratic future, fit for human beings.

In that spirit, I seek to offer in what follows an example of how Foster's work on regional policy has been used to frame our understanding of the deepening crisis of contemporary Scotland and how to engage with it in pursuit of a better future.

The health of the nation:
crystallising the trajectory of contemporary Scotland

The most telling way to crystallise the deeply troubling trajectory of contemporary Scotland is probably through the health of its population. Around 20 years ago, researchers were identifying the phenomenon of 'excess mortality' in Scotland – especially in the west of Scotland and particularly in Glasgow. Significantly more people were dying in these areas than would have been expected, even after taking account of poverty and deprivation. Stark health inequalities were an important part of the overall picture, but the heightened mortality affected the whole population. Importantly, the phenomenon had attained problematic proportions in the closing two decades of the twentieth century.[2]

The researchers struggled to find an adequate explanation, and this was reflected in the terminology they deployed. The 'Scottish Effect' and 'Glasgow

Effect' in health were ways of saying: 'something is happening with population health in these places that we cannot adequately explain'. By 2016, however, there was a substantial consensus around the explanation, which was heavily informed by the account of contemporary Scotland produced over the preceding decades by John Foster.[3]

Explaining Scotland's 'excess mortality': from 'the aftershock of deindustrialisation' to neoliberal 'political attack'

The explanation for the 'excess mortality' came in two main stages. Researchers had hypothesised that deindustrialisation in the Scottish context might be the explanation. But they found that in other parts of the UK and Europe, where deindustrialisation had been at least as evident – and poverty and deprivation perhaps even worse – the health improvement of the population had not been so adversely affected.[4]

Drawing heavily on Foster's account of contemporary Scotland, the first stage was to show that Scotland's excess mortality was linked to the neoliberal 'political attack' against the organised working class implemented by the post-1979 Conservative governments.[5] Through this 'attack', the UK as a whole was exposed to a rapid, severe and politically driven form of deindustrialisation, less managed and in its harmful consequences also less mitigated than was seen elsewhere in Europe. Foster's work was crucial in showing how Scotland – and especially the West of Scotland – became a particular target for the attack planned by the Conservative strategists prior to 1979.[6]

Foster's analysis of regional policy was writ large in all of this. It showed how the new international alignments after 1945 had led to the previously powerful leaders of Scottish heavy industry losing much of their influence at a UK level. Increasingly, the development of the Scottish economy (and indeed Scottish society) was to be shaped by external agendas – especially those of big business at UK level. As summarised by Foster:

> The maintenance of sterling as a world banking currency and the adoption of Keynesian economics demanded an alliance with the US. This in turn meant promoting the growth of multinational firms that were sufficiently large and competitive to survive within the US trading area. These firms operated at a UK level. They were mainly financed from the City of London and were primarily in motors, petrochemicals and electrical engineering.[7]

One outcome was that, initially, the leaders of Scottish heavy industry found themselves obliged to tolerate an influx of American owned branch plants, competing with them for labour and other key resources. These plants, central to the US's plans for the stabilisation of Europe, had been directed northwards to avoid them competing with more strategically important UK-level concerns. Within Scotland, they were directed to the emerging 'new towns'. The result was 'two largely separate economies' – and with that, the loss of any coherent perspective on the development of the economy around areas of indigenous industrial strength and potential.[8]

However, post-Suez, the previously strained tolerance between the leaders of the dual economies gave way to overt animosity – as a much strengthened regional policy pursued the 'modernisation' of Scotland via further external investment into a growing number of new towns and other designated 'growth areas'. Crucially, the policy makers also designated the older, heavy industries, and the areas in which they were located, as 'declining', and, as a matter of policy, specifically accelerated their decline.

All of this led to 'deep and long-lasting divisions within the country's political elite' – the dual economies duly went to 'war'.[9] It was also yet more highly damaging for the coherent development of the Scottish economy. Ultimately, the new jobs created in the 'modernised' sector fell far short of those lost in the older industries, and they also proved not to be very durable.

But the developments also set the scene for the emergence in the early 1970s of a broadly based movement, led by the working class but mobilising a much broader social alliance. This movement exploited the divisions within the ruling elite and sought to defend and redevelop what was left of the older industrial infrastructure – but on the kind of democratic basis which was an anathema to the whole ruling elite.

The movement took shape around the first attempt by a British government to pursue a neoliberal agenda – the 'Selsdon Agenda' of the Heath Government, elected in 1970. The focal point of the movement was the campaign for 'the right to work' led by the workers of Upper Clyde Shipbuilders – a government-backed consortium of four shipyards, which was targeted by the Heath government, initially for closure, and later for partial closure, with a reduction from 8,500 workers to just 2,500. The ensuing 'work-in', led by a co-ordinating committee of shop stewards, lasted over a year (1971-72). It not only succeeded in keeping all four yards in operation; it also played a vital part in forcing Heath's infamous U-turn – an effective abandonment of the prior neoliberal policy agenda and a return to a then more familiar form of social democratic consensualism. The 'work-in' harnessed the resentment of the many small and medium sized firms that stood to lose from the government enforced liquidation, and so produced a pointed challenge to the basic legitimacy of the neoliberal, pro-big business agenda driving it. The Government conceded to the UCS workers in order to preserve its larger commitment to big business at the UK level.

For a period, it seemed possible, based on this 'anti-monopoly alliance', that a regionally accountable democratic planning might emerge in Scotland.

However, by the turn of the decade something quite different was being imposed. This was to be a much more concerted version of neoliberal monetarism, framed by a reinvigorated right wing of the Conservative Party in response to the perceived humiliation of Heath's U-turn.

The organised and politically confident working class of Scotland was seen to have done much to force Heath's U-turn. Consequently, the neoliberal strategists paid close attention to the material underpinnings of this confidence – full employment, high levels of trade union membership in large industrial concerns, and the broader security offered by the welfare state, including large-scale council housing with its security of tenure and subsidised rents.[10] The neoliberal 'solution' was to plan carefully for the implementation of a sustained attack on all of these. Christopher Harvie was later to call it 'sado-monetarism'.[11] It had an impact across the UK but the most serious impact – as indicated by the population health outcomes – was in Scotland. A telling indicator of the special vulnerability to the attack in the Scottish context was the disproportionate increase after 1979, especially in the west of Scotland and Glasgow, of deaths arising from alcohol, drugs, suicide and violence – later to be labelled as 'deaths of despair'.[12]

In this way, John Foster's work provided the essential underpinning for grasping the political dynamic which had driven the sharp increase in Scotland's excess mortality in the closing decades of the twentieth century.

Understanding Scotland's special vulnerability to neoliberal political attack

But how, more specifically, had the special vulnerability to the damaging impacts of this neoliberal political attack been created in the Scottish context? This brings us to the second stage of the explanation. Here too, Foster's analysis proved vital, again focused on the impacts of regional policy, and at this stage especially in relation to Glasgow.

In this connection, Foster's work had clearly emphasised the quite staggering scale of the ambition of the policy makers in pursuing their agenda for the 'modernisation' of Scotland from the early 1960s, and the breadth of the social and geographical implications which it entailed. He had emphasised 'the explicitness with which the policy makers justified a fairly root and branch destruction of the old industrial infrastructure' and also the fact that 'all aspects of society were affected'.[13]

Nowhere was worse affected than Glasgow. Here, notably, Foster invokes Alasdair Gray's remarkable novel, *Lanark*, as conveying both the suddenness of the harmful impacts, and also the subjection which underlay them: '*Lanark* portrays Glasgow as a twentieth-century version of hell... the city is subsiding, sunless, without time. Its residents are progressively diseased. As they inexplicably disappear, their bodies are recycled – to provide heat and food for "The Institute" located somewhere else, possibly near New Cumbernauld'.[14]

Based on Foster's analysis, a new phase of research was conducted to provide a fuller explanation of the vulnerability underlying the emergence of the 'excess mortality' phenomenon in Scotland, particularly focused on Glasgow. This work drew heavily on Scottish Office documents and it revealed that even within a few years of embarking on their regional policy 'modernisation' agenda, policy makers were aware that their ambitions for a 'new Scotland' were looking unlikely to be fulfilled. They were also fully aware that the pursuit of their ambitions was having very damaging effects on Glasgow and Glaswegians. As the city's industries were forced into decline, there was a highly selective process of 'redeployment' of population, and especially of skilled labour, from the city to the new towns and other designated 'growth areas'. These areas were also the priorities for public investment to create high amenity, balanced and attractive communities.

Glasgow could not be allocated anything like the same priority for its retained population. Indeed, quite the reverse. The wholesale clearance and demolition which took place in the older city saw the retained population dispersed to remote peripheral estates, with poor quality house types, ill-conceived high-rise blocks and expensive public transport links. The amenities provided, in contrast to the designated 'growth areas', were woefully inadequate – and often virtually non-existent. All of this was done under the close supervision and scrutiny of the Scottish Office. Glasgow's own scope for initiative had been very heavily diminished.

By 1971, civil servants in Edinburgh were concerned that in terms of Glasgow their policies were 'destined within a decade or so to produce a seriously unbalanced population with a very high proportion of the old, the very poor and the almost unemployable' – with all the predictable social consequences. However, despite reaching the view that 'probably no other city can display quite such depressing prospects', the policy makers concluded that there was little 'room for manoeuvre' – that the scale of the commitment to the 'modernisation' agenda precluded measures for Glasgow beyond those which would mitigate some of the worst symptoms of that agenda. Several years later, even the purposive intervention of a Glasgow MP, Bruce Millan, as Secretary of State for Scotland, was to prove insufficient to alter these investment and growth priorities – which were to prevail until the early years of the new millennium.[15]

By that time the 'depressing prospects' which policy makers had anticipated in early 1971 were being crystallised in the phenomenon of 'excess mortality' that was being identified by researchers. At the same time, the Scottish electronics and computing sector – very much the 'success story' of the regional policy 'modernisation' agenda – was seeing output fall by half, amidst a wave of closures and contractions. These partly reflected a global recession, but also the fact that the shallow roots of the external firms involved facilitated a shift in production towards lower cost locations in Eastern Europe and Asia.[16] It is unsurprising, then, that in this context the 'excess mortality' phenomenon was to continue to grow in the years ahead.[17]

The tremendous utility of Foster's work is in enabling us to see these phenomena as inextricably linked expressions of the stark economic and social vulnerability which had been created in Scotland by a profoundly misconceived regional policy 'modernisation' agenda. It was an agenda which was pursued over at least four decades, with a high degree of commitment, if not ruthlessness, serving primarily the needs of British business at UK level. Much that was of actual and potential economic value was deliberately destroyed in pursuit of a 'Brigadoon' of 'modernisation'. There was no Plan B.

The effects were deeply disintegrative, as exhibited very clearly on Clydeside (though by no means only there). As Foster put it, already in 2003, the cumulative outcomes of four decades of 'modernisation' meant that 'the incidence of illness and mortality is the worst in Western Europe'.[18]

With this, Foster had put his finger on the essential causal relationship between regional policy and 'excess mortality', even as the latter phenomenon was still in the process of being identified. The work that was subsequently done to explain the phenomenon was in many ways explicating the distressing detail of a causal relationship which Foster had already identified.

At the root of the phenomenon had been two main factors. Firstly, there had been the subordination of the economic and social development of Scotland to external agendas, serving external needs, leading to the loss of indigenous ownership and control – and, with that, to deepening economic and social vulnerability. And secondly, there had been the failure to build a democratic platform able to interrogate those external agendas, ideally with the powers to develop the economy directly, and at least able to counter more effectively the forces of social and economic disintegration.

From 'lagging health improvement' to declining population health

However, by the time that the 'excess mortality' phenomenon was being more fully explained, in 2016, the population health trend in Scotland was worsening. In the preceding period, 'excess mortality' had reflected the fact that population health was *improving more slowly* in Scotland and Glasgow than in comparison areas. But by 2013, population health improvement across the UK – including Scotland – was slowing. Shortly thereafter, average life expectancy in Scotland was *falling*. The trends for some groups were much worse – with, for instance, rapid deterioration in mortality rates, life expectancy and healthy life expectancy in the poorest communities in Glasgow.[19]

These developments are unprecedented in modern times. Neither the 'hungry thirties' nor the brutal recessions of the closing decades of the twentieth century brought with them such declines in overall population health. Importantly, the recent developments were not set in motion by the Covid-19 pandemic and in fact preceded them by several years. Instead, as the research clearly shows, they have been fundamentally driven by the austerity imposed by UK governments in the aftermath of the 2008 banking crisis and the ensuing 'great recession'. While the developments are not restricted to Scotland, in the Scottish context they build, as we have seen, on an already deeply problematic inheritance.

One prominent reaction has been indignation: 'these developments should not be happening in a wealthy, democratic society'; 'politicians have failed to act in the required ways and must now do so', and so on. This is an understandable reaction; but it begs more questions than it answers: questions precisely about the wealth of our society, and how it is produced, owned and shared; questions precisely about our democracy, and how far it is able to serve the needs and interests of people in our society.

If we are to return our troubled nation to an improving trajectory in population health, and to secure meaningful and sustained reductions in those appalling, and currently worsening, health inequalities, then these are the questions which need answered. In answering them, researchers will find themselves greatly assisted by the continuing, indispensable analysis of the development of the economy and society in Scotland which has been provided by Foster over the past twenty years. Many of these outputs are listed in the bibliography of his work, which is to be found at the end of this book. The most fitting recognition of the value of these contributions will be to use them as a part of the ongoing efforts to understand Scotland's current crisis, and to orientate the progressive forces in our society in their struggle to create a better future.

As Foster has put it very recently: 'The magnitude of the present challenge means we have to think about how poverty, inequality and the private ownership of productive assets (mostly now external) can be challenged, as it was in founding days of the labour movement, by united action and solidarity based both in trade unions and communities'.[20]

Notes

1   'Paisley Tech', as it was known, is now part of the University of the West of Scotland.
2   P. Hanlon, R.S. Lawder, D. Buchanan, et al, 'Why is mortality higher in Scotland than in England and Wales?', Journal of Public Health, 27 (2005), 199-204; D. Walsh, M. Taulbut, and P. Hanlon, *The aftershock of deindustrialisation: Trends in mortality in Scotland and other parts of post-industrial Europe*, Glasgow Centre for Population Health: 2008); D. Walsh, N. Bendel, R. Jones and P. Hanlon, 'It's not "just deprivation": Why do equally deprived UK cities experience different health outcomes?' Public Health, 124 (2010), 487–495; D. Walsh, G. McCartney, C. Collins, M. Taulbut and G.D. Batty, *History, politics and vulnerability: Explaining excess mortality in Scotland and Glasgow* (Glasgow Centre for Population Health, Glasgow: 2016)
3   Walsh et al., *History, politics and vulnerability*.
4   Walsh et al., *Aftershock*.
5   See especially J. Foster and C. Woolfson, *The Politics of the UCS Work-In: Class Alliances and the Right to Work* (Lawrence and Wishart, London: 1986); J. Foster, 'The Twentieth Century, 1914-1979', in R. A. Houston and W. W. J. Knox (eds), *The New Penguin History of Scotland: From the Earliest Times to the Present Day* (Allen Lane in association with the National Museums of Scotland, London: 2001), 417-96; J. Foster, 'The Economic Restructuring of the West of Scotland 1945-2000', in G. Blazyca (ed.), *Restructuring of Regional Economies: Towards a Comparative Study of Scotland and Upper Silesia* (Ashgate Press, Aldershot: 2003), 57-69.
6   C. Collins and G. McCartney, 'The Impact of Neoliberal "Political Attack" on Health: The Case of the "Scottish Effect"', *International Journal of Health Services*, 41 (2011), 501-523.
7   Foster, 'Economic Restructuring', 61.
8   Foster, 'Economic Restructuring', 62.
9   Foster, 'Twentieth Century', 468; J. Foster, 'The Economic Restructuring', 65.
10 Foster and Woolfson, *UCS Work-In*, Ch.10, esp. 401-404; Foster, 'The Economic Restructuring', esp. 65-66.
11 C. Harvie, *Scotland: A Short History* (Oxford University Press, Oxford: 2002), 213.
12 Walsh et al., 'It's not "just deprivation"'.
13 Foster, 'Economic Restructuring', 63; Foster, 'Twentieth Century', 471.
14 Foster, 'Twentieth Century', 472.
15 C. Collins and I. Levitt, 'The "Modernisation" of Scotland and its Impact on Glasgow, 1955-1979: "Unwanted Side effects" and Vulnerabilities', *Scottish Affairs* 25 (2016), 294-316; C. Collins and I. Levitt, 'The policy discourses that shaped the "transformation" of Glasgow in the later twentieth century: "Overspill", "redeployment" and the "culture of enterprise", in K. Kintrea and R. Madgin (eds), *Transforming Glasgow: Beyond the Post-Industrial City* (Policy Press, Bristol: 2020), 21-38.
16 I. Turok and N. Bailey, 'Glasgow's Recent Trajectory', in D. Newlands, M. Danson and J. McCarthy (eds), *Divided Scotland?* (Ashgate, Aldershot: 2004), 35-59.
17 Walsh et al., *History, politics and vulnerability*.
18 Foster, 'Economic Restructuring', 66.
19 G. McCartney, D. Walsh, L. Fenton, and R. Devine, *Resetting the Course for Population Health* (Glasgow Centre for Population Health/University of Glasgow, Glasgow: 2022); G. McCartney, D. Walsh, L. Fenton, and R. Devine, *Changing Mortality Rates in Scotland and the UK* (Glasgow Centre for Population Health, Glasgow: 2022).
20 J. Foster, 'The Coming Cuts to Public Spending', *ROSE: Radical Options for Scotland and Europe*, 1 (2024), 5-7.

3 ROGER SEIFERT

Workplace struggles: class conflict as it happened

Introduction

THE CENTRE OF class struggle is, from time to time, found in workplaces, and the nature of that conflict and its outcome provides a clue as to the balance of class forces in the wider community. Notions of solidarity are part of such a calculus.[1] The starting point for any social and historical study of real-world phenomena is the evidence before us. Materialism requires a clear-sighted view of what happens, and dialectics allows such 'facts' to be understood within the context of history, political economy of the moment, and the clash of class forces. The way of history is thus seen as an attack on oppression through a determined class struggle (revolution) and not through peaceful negotiation (reform).[2] In this account, therefore, the everyday working lives of all members of the working class are the starting point – always begin at the beginning. The experience of exploitation and alienation, although hidden from view, comes to the surface and finds form in acts of dissent. When such dissent articulates general discontent and is made viable through the collective of trade unionism, then and only then, does apparent conflict become real struggle. Consciousness can then be shifted through both the mechanics of the conflict and the injection of wider objectives that challenge the rights of management to manage and those of owners to freely exercise their prerogatives.

The traditional Marxist analysis of all societies is that the engine of change is class conflict. In the modern era, this usually, but not exclusively, refers to clashes of interests as between landowners, capitalists, and workers. This is an objective reality and relates to ownership and control of resources. The ways in which these 'worldly goods' are distributed depends on both objective economic conditions of any nation state aided and abetted by political and military powers; and by the agency of those directly involved – workers, their allies, and their organisations.

This idealised form of class struggle becomes concrete in workplace conflicts with the 'drudge day' tensions over everything that matters relating to wages, hours, health and safety; bullying and discrimination; victimisation of union activists; and, *inter alia*, training, promotion, and job security.[3] Dealing with such issues indicates both a common cause and the potential to raise trade union consciousness into class consciousness. G.D.H. Cole explained: 'Trade unionism... was really born in the troublous days of the French Wars and the Industrial Revolution', because 'for the first time political and industrial ideas began powerfully to interact'.[4]

The application of these tools of analysis to the workplace is the task of historians and social scientists. Commentary always matters, and more so in the age of fast and vast news outlets. It is important to bear witness to events, especially ones which illustrate the class nature of society and the embedded use of exploitation as a means of suppression. Struggle, therefore, takes place in the domain of the workplace but also in the realm of reporting and understanding its meaning. A central aspect is the distinction between a revolutionary socialist perspective rooted in Marxism-Leninism and the world of reformism associated with compromise within a supported capitalist system in which British imperialism helped British workers to benefit from the exploitation of others.[5] It is struggle and political agitation that wins and loses the battle for ideas within the context of the workplace. Here, detailed historical and contemporary studies contribute to both collective memory and the benefits for future struggles of the trial and error of past battles.[6]

As Hobsbawm notes, 'My object is to understand and explain why things turned out the way they did, and how they hang together'.[7] This formed the basis for the approach taken by other Marxist social historians towards industrial disputes, whether in the USA in the 1870s or in Scotland in the 1970s, and with that comes the ability to deliver the necessary guides to revolution.[8]

Upper Clyde Shipbuilders

Bert Ramelson, the Communist Party's industrial organiser, understood these pressures and tensions and helped build on the successes of strikes in the late 1960s which allowed radical new approaches to protect jobs. A major example was the breakthrough, innovative and landmark struggle at Upper Clyde Shipbuilders (UCS) in the summer of 1971.[9] The context, familiar to millions of workers, was that the company had failed to modernise; real economic pressures from overseas competitors were ignored; and the senior management were self-serving and secretive. In addition, the new Conservative government was replete with dogmatic capitalist libertarians, who refused to accept the end of empire, and who took advice from vested interests with the deepest pockets. Such a setting was not conducive to any strategic settlement, and the labour movement leadership, dominated by reformist-minded social democrats, began to wash their hands of the whole mess while espousing platitudes of regret.

Only the workers, their own shop stewards and local union leaders, allied with powerful left forces and high-profile political figures, decided to act. Inspired by the desperate needs of the hour, learning from historical struggles, aware of the Scottish dimension, and blessed with high energy and engaging communication skills, they (Jimmy Reid, Jimmy Airlie, Sammy Barr – all members of the Communist Party) plumped for a work-in that drew international attention to their demands.[10]

Foster and Woolfson provided the necessary account of this totemic struggle with a mixture of historical awareness, first-hand accounts from the main protagonists, a Marxist class-based analysis, and a detailed rapportage of events, decisions, and context.[11] The outcome was a blueprint for large-scale workplace struggles, as class conflict was brought to every worker's front door and backroom.

This case study, in addition to its worth as an account of events themselves, acts as a clear finger pointing to the exploitation of those involved, as well as the alienation created by the power imbalance and nature of the division of labour. It shines a light on the basics of historical materialism and develops the relationship between consciousness and being that allows a dialectic reasoning to uncover relations otherwise obscured.[12] In this sense the case of UCS provides a model for others to follow.

The analysis is the result of a deep knowledge of the history of struggle and its chronicling as the dots of our complex world are joined up. Earlier breakthrough studies by Hobsbawm, Saville, and Thompson showed the way, but the signposts have to be read and followed. The UCS study does this and concludes: 'Taking the UCS struggle as a whole and turning to the wider political lessons, three points may finally be singled out. The first concerns leadership: the need for a vanguard that is theoretically strong and rooted within the decisive sections of the working class... The second concerns the character of the workers among whom the vanguard must be based... the third conclusion... concerns the nature of alliances.'[13]

Tracing class struggle at work

Lenin in his proactive and practical manner sought out those sections of the working class after the Russian Revolution that could form vanguard parties in countries such as Britain. This meant the creation of a Communist Party and with it a focus on the most revolutionary elements of the class. Some of this emerged from workplace struggles, especially where such places were huge collectives of workers, highly unionised, volatile, and open to radical change. Marxist historians have drawn upon such bases since G.D.H. Cole and Robin Page Arnot, to keep track of the shifting sands of class identity and the impact upon trade union programmes, and how struggle is both cause and effect of political awakenings. Case studies such as UCS, the Shrewsbury pickets, and the Pentonville Five merge the detailed story of the dynamics of each struggle with the contradictory nature of fighting within the narrow confines of capitalist property relations, and furthermore onto the larger stage of national and international class conflict.[14]

Strikes and action short of strikes are the most visible form and shape of workplace strife. While there have been numerous accounts of individual strikes and important works on their general nature, the most powerful case studies are those, like Foster and Woolfson's, that combine the strikes' causes and conduct with the wider class struggle, analyse employer and state responses, and provide a systematic view of the consequences for those involved in the wider movement.

Interlocking historical studies of struggles at the workplace and beyond, alongside political demands, form the dialectic of struggle built upon the foundation stones of the nature of exploitation under capitalism – the extraction of surplus value in the production process. This in turn requires such inequity to be hidden from view through the complex and ever-changing constructs of social and economic life depicted through cultural channels, and ruling by dividing the working class, undermining struggle legally and ideologically, and shifting the frontier of control at work in favour of employers.[15]

In such schemes, notions of solidarity, that unity is strength, become urgent calls for resistance, and are cynically undermined by both the class enemy and those inside the labour movement bent on traducing militancy. A world of workplace struggle in which the only defence of terms and conditions, job security, and bilaterally determined wages, is trade unionism, is one that needs tactical flexibility, a coalition of forces, and leadership. Case studies illustrate this for the past to better inform the present and the future.[16]

The ways in which Bert Ramelson worked with key trade-union allies to build solidarity and establish – with Kevin Halpin – the Liaison Committee for the Defence of Trade Unions is a testament to this kind of working.[17] They developed key cadres inside the unions; built upon justified discontent among union members; created a strategic network; and made a difference to some of the great battles of the time. In this, the detail of conflict at all levels of struggle, from incomes policies through employers' offensives to the grain of day-to-day working practices, was the material base for organising union resistance, raising consciousness, and holding the class together as a class 'of' and 'for itself'. The siren calls of division based on sex, ethnicity, age, skill, region, religion, and nationality were rebuffed by the common cause and the strength of a one-dimensional purpose. The basis upon which the working class is identified as both a class of and for itself and as the prime identifier for revolutionary struggles does not reduce other struggles for equality, but rather enhances them as embracing the widest common denominator within capitalist society – those who survive as a group through selling their only possession, their labour power.

Conclusion

The role of trade union history as a subset of working-class history formally began in the UK with the Webbs.[18] Marxists and others used these analytical categories to stratify the working class as a class, to develop the notion of class consciousness over and above trade union consciousness, and to explain policy and political proclivities among such sections. The ideal of a labour aristocracy took corporeal form through association with craft unions and their support for highly protectionist trade arrangements including colonialism.

While too many trade union histories were written from the narrow perspective of leaders and senior officials with a dry account of formal proceedings, there has been a real shift in recent years to more dynamic accounts of trade unions as vehicles of struggle, both local and national. Such volumes allow insight into the nuts and bolts of trade unionism in workplace conflicts, association with local community causes, and in playing its part at national level. The recent history of the TGWU in collaboration with Unite and the Marx Memorial Library is one example of a class-based analysis of a dynamic workers' organisation.[19]

The twin familiar calls that history is written by the victors and that the first casualty of war is truth, both siding with the Marxist dictum that at any time the ruling ideas are those of the ruling class, bring together the efforts to hide from history the true nature of class society.[20] This is countered by both the reality of the totality of working-class lived experiences, and by those that tell the tale. A tale related through time, with many voices: 'The Marxist historical method is able to demonstrate its superiority most powerfully in the sphere of contemporary history, where judgements are most rapidly and mercilessly brought to the test of subsequent events'.[21] Bert Ramelson was a leading exponent of this 'class conflict as it happened' and relied on accounts of the UCS work-in and others to inform and develop an industrial strategy to keep the march of labour going forward.

'The history of the trade union movement, of workers' struggles as members of the working class, is part of all history'.[22] It is 'a dialogue between the events of the past and progressively emerging future ends'.[23] This Enlightenment perspective on interpretation underlined the relevance of the historians' task, 'what they [Florentine historians of the early 1500s] most desired was, that their view of the course of events should have as wide and deep a practical effect as possible'.[24] The relevance today in 2024, a year after the largest strike wave this century, is clear in terms of attacks from all sides on the strikers, efforts to delegitimise trade unionism as a representative body, the silencing of left arguments and protests, and despite Brexit, becoming part of Fortress Europe with the rise of the far right amongst sections of the working class.[25]

Notes

1   J. Foster, *Class Struggle and the Industrial Revolution: Early Industrial Capitalism in Three English Towns* (Weidenfeld and Nicolson, London: 1974); V.L. Allen, *Trade Union Leadership: Based on a Study of Arthur Deakin* (Longmans, Green & Co., London: 1957).

2   G.A. Cohen, *Karl Marx's Theory of History: A Defence* (Clarendon Press, Oxford: 1978), 25.

3   K. Marx, 'The Eighteenth Brumaire of Louis Napoleon', *Selected Works*, Vol. 1, (Progress Publishers, Moscow, 1969), 394-487; E. Hobsbawm, *Primitive Rebels* (Manchester University Press, Manchester: 1959); J. Foster, 'Karl Marx Oration 2018', *Theory & Struggle*, 118 (2018), 133-6, and, 'Marx and the British Working Class', *Theory & Struggle*, 120 (2019), 2-9; S. Tolliday, and J. Zeitlin (eds), *Shop Floor Bargaining and the State* (Cambridge University Press, Cambridge: 1985).

4   G.D.H Cole, *Organised Labour* (Allen & Unwin, London: 1924), 1-2.

5   V.L. Lenin, *Imperialism the Highest Form of Capitalism* (Martin Lawrence, London: 1933).

6   J. Foster, 'How Oldham's Working-Class Leaders Managed to Avoid Reformism, 1812-1847', *Bulletin of the Society for the Study of Labour History*, 16: (1968), 6-10; and, 'Revolutionaries in Oldham', *Marxism Today*: (Nov. 1968), 335- 43; H. Braverman, *Labor and Monopoly Capital* (Monthly Review Press, New York: 1974).

7   E. Hobsbawm, *Age of Extremes: The Short Twentieth Century, 1914-1991* (Michael Joseph, London: 1994), 3.

8   P. Foner, *The Great Labor Uprising of 1877* (Pathfinder, New York: 1977); J. Foster, 'Eric Hobsbawm: A Marxist who Transformed the Writing of History', *Labour History Review*, 78, 3 (2013), 351-71; and, 'Eric Hobsbawm, Marxism and Social History', *Social History*, 39, 2: (2014), 160-171.

9   W. Thompson, and F. Hart, *The UCS Work-In* (Lawrence & Wishart, London: 1972).

10 W. Knox, and A. McKinlay, *Jimmy Reid: A Clyde-Built Man* (Liverpool University Press, Liverpool: 2019).

11 J. Foster and C. Woolfson, *The Politics of the UCS Work-in: Class Alliances and the Right to Work* (Lawrence & Wishart, London: 1986).

12 K. Marx, 'Preface to the Contribution to the Critique of Political Economy', *Selected Works*, Vol. 1 (Progress Publishers, Moscow: 1969), 502-6.

13 Foster and Woolfson, *UCS*, 427.

14 R. Seifert and T. Sibley, *Revolutionary Communist at Work: A Political Biography of Bert Ramelson* (Lawrence & Wishart, London: 2012); R. Darlington and D. Lyddon, *Glorious Summer: Class Struggle in Britain 1972* (Bookmarks, London: 2001).

15 A. Gramsci, *Prison Notebooks* (Lawrence & Wishart, London, 1971).

16 J. Foster, 'The 1919 Forty Hours Strike', *Theory & Struggle*, 121 (2020), 30-41; C. Goodrich, *The Frontier of Control: A Study in British Workshop Politics* (Harcourt, Brace and Howe, New York: 1920).

17 K. Halpin, *Memoirs of a Militant: Sharply and to the Point* (Praxis Press, Glasgow: 2012); R. Seifert, 'Social Contract or Con-trick?', in M. Davis (ed.), *A Centenary for Socialism* (Manifesto Press, London: 2020); 145-158.

18 S. Webb and B. Webb., *History of Trade Unionism 1666-1920* (Printed by the Authors: 1919).

19 *UNITE History Project: M. Davis, and J. Foster, Vol. 1 (1880-1931): The Transport and General Workers Union: Representing a Mass Trade Union Movement* (Liverpool University Press, Liverpool: 2022); R. Seifert, Vol. 2 (1932-1945) *'No Turning Back': The Road to War and Welfare* (Liverpool University Press, Liverpool: 2022); M. Mayo, Vol. 3 (1945-1960) *Post-War Britain: The Welfare State and the Cold War* (Liverpool University Press, Liverpool: 2022); J. Foster, Vol. 4 (1960-1974): *The Great Tradition of Independent Working Class Power*; (Liverpool, Liverpool University Press: 2023); M. Davis, Vol. 5 (1974-1992) *From Zenith to Nadir* (Liverpool, Liverpool University Press: 2023) A. Weir, Vol. 6 (1992-2010) *Unity for a New Era* (Liverpool University Press, Liverpool: 2023).

20 K. Marx and F. Engels, 'The German Ideology', *Selected Works*, Vol. 1 (Progress Publishers, Moscow, 1969).

21 R.P. Dutt, *Problems of Contemporary History* (International Publishers, New York: 1963), 16.

22 Seifert, *No Turning Back*, 154.

23 E.H. Carr, *What is History?* (Pelican Books, Harmondsworth: 1961), 123.

24 J. Burkhardt, *The Civilization of the Renaissance in Italy* (Phaidon Press, London, 1960 edition: 1860), 148.

25 J. Foster, 'Marx, Marxism and the British Working-Class Movement: Some Continuing Issues in the 21st Century', *World Review of Political Economy*, 2, 4 (2011), 671-86.

Classes, cultures and nations

THE INTER-RELATIONSHIP between class and national identities, the connection or conflict between socialism and nationalism, are issues that have tested Marxists for generations, both in theory and practice.

Are these concepts easily compatible or are they mutually exclusive? Has the development of capitalism as a global system rendered national struggles redundant or has the imperialist stage of capitalism intensified national conflicts? These are debates with more than a century behind them.

Few Marxists in Britain have contributed more to clarifying these questions than John Foster. No attempt is made here to examine in detail his many articles, book chapters and pamphlets which have tackled these questions head on in numerous political and academic fora over half a century. A glance at the bibliography at the end of this book suggests that would be an insurmountable challenge.

Unfortunately, this means leaving out most of Foster's important contributions on the emergence of the Scottish nation, as well as his voluminous work on the issues of national democracy and popular sovereignty in relation to the European Union. The focus instead is on Foster's insistence that it is the mainstream Marxist tradition, principally encompassing Marx and Engels themselves, as well as Lenin, Connolly and Dimitrov, which provides the most fruitful approach to 'answering the national question'.

Theoretical framework

One of the key Marxist aspects of approaches to the national question is where do nations come from, or perhaps better still, *when* do nations emerge? The second question is sometimes inaccurately answered as 'with the emergence of capitalism'. Foster, however, insists that this is mistaken. In his view, both Marx and Engels writing in the nineteenth century, and Lenin writing in the twentieth, acknowledged the existence of early forms of national identity and nationhood before their appropriation and consolidation in modern capitalist society.

From this perspective, 'nations' are neither eternal, ahistorical entities (a fundamental tenet of most national creation myths) nor simply a by-product of the creation of unified markets during the dissolution of feudalism and the emergence of the capitalist mode of production, alongside shifts toward national currencies, uniform property laws and standardised national languages.

Instead, national and ethnic social formations are constantly in process of re-creation and modification. They adapt to transformations of modes of production and the rise and fall of various class forces, vying to dominate the existing or emerging formations. The emergence of a fully-fledged modern nation is a matter of historical development, just as with their disappearance or absorption into other nations. Foster's most ambitious work, for example, was on the formation of Scotland, an unlikely amalgam of Picts, Celts, Anglo-Saxons and Norse peoples, forged by material conditions, class alliances, religious and ideological currents, and clashes of social systems – with early feudal Scots kingdoms pitted against slave-trading Vikings.[1]

While this does not mean that every pre-capitalist ethnic group can be categorised as 'national' or even proto-national, it does help to explain how pre-existing human, cultural, linguistic and even economic communities provided the foundations for modern nations.

Foster, much to the chagrin of his critics, has been one of the few post-1956 Marxist writers to acknowledge the insights of Soviet Marxists. One of these key influences was the late Soviet ethnographer Yulian Bromley, whose interpretation of 'ethnos' has particularly influenced Foster.[2] Bromley, drawing on both Soviet and international anthropological and ethnographical research, suggested that there was an obvious continuum between pre-capitalist communities and the modern capitalist nation. Ties of place, language, customs and religion often transcended the shift from one mode of production to another – this was also the case in the transitions experienced in the Soviet Union, particularly in Central Asia.

Bromley understood this community as an 'ethnos', not necessarily a nation in the modern or specifically Marxist sense, but a real human community. This 'ethnos' did not merely replicate itself biologically but also culturally. Yet at the same time, as with every class-based community, the ethnos would be transformed, reconfigured, even re-named, and re-made, because of both incremental social change as well as revolutionary ruptures with previous social formations. If capitalism made nations, what were the raw materials for its production and reproduction?

Foster argues that the Marxist approach:

...sees the contested definition of nationalities and national identities as inherent in the class-determined process of state formation, politico-economic change and the creation of revolutionary alliances. This is what Marx and Engels quite clearly argued in the *Communist Manifesto*. It is an approach that demands a concrete historical analysis – not one locked on by externally conceived stages that themselves predict the answer.[3]

'The workers have no country': Marx and Engels

Foster's reference to the *Manifesto of the Communist Party* may strike some as incongruous, after all the text famously contains what appears to be dismissal of the importance of the nation to the working class: 'The working men have no country. We cannot take from them what they have not got.'

However, Marx and Engels continue: 'Since the proletariat must first of all acquire political supremacy, must rise to be the leading class of the nation, must constitute itself the nation, it is so far, itself national, though not in the bourgeois sense of the word.'[4]

The *Manifesto* further brings out the processes underpinning the foundation of bourgeois 'nation-states':

> The bourgeoisie keeps more and more doing away with the scattered state of the population, of the means of production, and of property. It has agglomerated population, centralised the means of production, and has concentrated property in a few hands. The necessary consequence of this was political centralisation...

Yet at the same time:

> National differences and antagonism between peoples are daily more and more vanishing, owing to the development of the bourgeoisie, to freedom of commerce, to the world market, to uniformity in the mode of production and in the conditions of life corresponding thereto.
> The supremacy of the proletariat will cause them to vanish still faster. United action, of the leading civilised countries at least, is one of the first conditions for the emancipation of the proletariat.[5]

Internationalism is therefore incomprehensible without the recognition of these national factors. In the later *Grundrisse* (1857-58) and in the very late *Ethnological Notebooks* compiled in the last years of his life, Marx had been intrigued by the development of human society, moving beyond the bonds of family kinship, but not yet reaching the stage of nationhood or concepts of national identity. Likewise, Engels' *Origin of the Family, Private Property and the State* (1884) had also set out to analyse the varieties of social communities that existed in pre-capitalist societies. As Foster explains:

> Throughout his writings, Marx explored the emergence of ethnic social formations: from the tribe and clan to the first slave-based class societies, to feudalism and the revolutionary creation of the capitalist nation. In this process, Marx presents nationalities and nations as being transformed – and sometimes entirely new nations being created – as each new ruling class puts in place the state power requirements for each new mode of production. The class that was progressive at one stage would be

reactionary at the next. Accordingly, the history and culture of nations always had to be analysed concretely in terms of the class forces that successively moulded them.[6]

Lenin on national democracy and culture

The second theoretical contribution which Foster draws upon is that of Lenin. Russian Marxists were faced with the practical problem of how to reconcile the struggle for socialism with the fact that the arena in which it took place, the Tsarist Empire, was a 'prison of the peoples'. Lenin also closely followed the debates within European Social-Democracy, polemicising against those on the revolutionary left who he felt underestimated the importance of the national issue, such as Rosa Luxemburg, and others like the Austro-Marxist, Otto Bauer, who expressed revisionist and reformist solutions. He wrote in 1913:

The *elements* of democratic and socialist culture are present, if only in rudimentary form, in every national culture, since in every nation there are toiling and exploited masses, whose conditions of life inevitably give rise to the ideology of democracy and socialism. But every nation also possesses a bourgeois culture (and most nations a reactionary and clerical culture as well) in the form, not merely of 'elements', but of the *dominant* culture.[7]

This was a point Lenin returned to with some passion soon after the opening of the First World War, when he argued that the defeat of Tsarism was in the best interests of the peoples of the Russian Empire, even including the dominant national group:

We are full of national pride because the Great-Russian nation, too, has created a revolutionary class, because it, too, has proved capable of providing mankind with great models of the struggle for freedom and socialism, and not only with great pogroms, rows of gallows, dungeons, great famines and great servility to priests, tsars, landowners and capitalists.[8]

The war also accelerated his own thinking on imperialism as a special stage of capitalism that divided the world into two main camps, oppressing nations and oppressed ones. Again, he found himself at odds with some of his fellow anti-war revolutionaries, who now argued that imperialism transcended 'the obsolete ideal of national states'.

Criticising Karl Radek, Lenin said that, on the contrary:

Imperialism means that capital has outgrown the framework of national states; it means that national oppression has been extended and heightened on a new historical foundation. Hence, it follows that... we must link the revolutionary struggle for socialism with a revolutionary programme on the national question.[9]

Other influences

This leap, resulting from Lenin's deepened analysis of imperialism, may explain the inadequacies of another seminal text, namely Joseph Stalin's *Marxism and the National Question*, written in 1913. Here Stalin outlined his criteria for nationhood:

> A nation is a historically evolved, stable community of language, territory, economic life, and psychological make-up manifested in a community of culture.
>
> It goes without saying that a nation, like every other historical phenomenon, is subject to the law of change, has its history, its beginning and end.
>
> It must be emphasised that none of the above characteristics is by itself sufficient to define a nation. On the other hand, it is sufficient for a single one of these characteristics to be lacking and the nation ceases to be a nation.[10]

The pamphlet was welcomed by Lenin and its focus on then – current European realities – particularly those national entities still within the Austro-Hungarian, Ottoman and Tsarist empires – still has historical resonance. However, at that point the Leninist concept of imperialism had not been fully developed and it was this theory, combined with the actual experience of imperialist war, which in turn generated the embrace of the national liberation movements of Asia and Africa that were to become central concerns of the Communist International.

In his critical review of Neil Davidson's *The Origins of Scottish Nationhood* (2000), Foster noted that despite the author's own avowed anti-Stalinism, the book's 'rather mechanical definitions' ironically mirrored some of Stalin's errors, namely that: 'Stalin similarly set class and nation conceptually apart. He made nationhood a function of capitalism and denied political legitimacy to pre-capitalist national formations.'[11] Although Foster noted that Stalin had later (1923) revised his earlier formulations in line with Lenin's insight that imperialism had created an entire category of oppressed nations.

Among these oppressed nations and central to the concerns of Marxists in Britain, was of course Ireland. Given Foster's personal connection to the island it is perhaps not surprising that the work of James Connolly and in particular his most famous maxim, 'The cause of labour is the cause of Ireland, the cause of Ireland is the cause of labour. They cannot be dissevered', is included in Foster's Communist Party pamphlet *Nations and Working-Class Unity in Britain* (2023). Nevertheless, he was at pains to make clear that Ireland's status as a victim of British colonialism and imperialism is quite distinct from that of the nations of Britain; Scotland, Wales and England.[12]

Yet, Connolly's contribution, which ultimately cost him his life at the hands of a British firing squad, was rooted in an internationalist class perspective, as might be expected of an Edinburgh-born revolutionary whose agitation took him across Britain and to the United States.

The final influential figure is Georgi Dimitrov. A veteran of the Bulgarian socialist movement, Dimitrov had famously faced down his Nazi accusers at his 1933 Leipzig trial over the Reichstag fire. He exposed the chauvinism of the Nazis, mocking their bogus racial theories of Aryan superiority over the supposedly unsophisticated Slavs:

> Our political struggle, our political aspirations are no less lofty than those of other peoples. A people which lived for five hundred years under a foreign yoke without losing its language and its national character, our working class and peasantry who have fought and are fighting against Bulgarian fascism and for communism – such a people is not savage and barbarous. Only fascism in Bulgaria is savage and barbarous. But I ask you, *in what country does not fascism bear these qualities?*[13]

In his main report to the Communist International's Seventh World Congress in 1935, which was devoted to ending the previous left-sectarian strategies and adopting the United Front Against Fascism and War, Dimitrov warned delegates that the fascists were successfully 'rummaging' through the history and culture of nations for their own ends. The contrast between the democratic and the reactionary national cultures now took on an even more deadly form:

> Mussolini does his utmost to make capital for himself out of the heroic figure of Garibaldi. The French fascists bring to the fore as their heroine Joan of Arc...
> Communists who suppose that all this has nothing to do with the cause of the working class, who do nothing to enlighten the masses on the past of their people in a historically correct fashion, in a genuinely Marxist-Leninist spirit, who do nothing to *link up the present struggle with the people's revolutionary traditions and past* – voluntarily hand over to the fascist falsifiers all that is valuable in the historical past of the nation, so that the fascists may fool the masses.[14]

Finally, Dimitrov urged an end to the indifference and even hostility to popular national feelings, arguing that this in fact stood in the way of raising and broadening political class consciousness:

> The task of educating the workers and all working people in the spirit of proletarian internationalism is one of the fundamental tasks of every Communist Party. But anyone who thinks that this permits him, or even compels him, to sneer at all the national sentiments of the broad masses of working people is far from being a genuine Bolshevik and has understood nothing of the teaching of Lenin on the national question.[15]

Lessons for the future

John Foster's approach, rooted in the classics of Marxism, provides a dynamic and dialectical means of understanding the creation and constant re-fashioning of national identity, based on the shifting balance of class forces. It is this approach which informs, for example, his championing of 'progressive federalism' based on the 'collective class strength of the great majority of the peoples of Britain, offering an alternative to the Anglo-centric (although perhaps Home Counties-centric is more apt) conceptions of Britishness that currently dominate both Labour and Tory parties, as well as acting as a counter to the separatist arguments that seek to tie legitimate national aspirations to Nato's war alliance or a fantastical 'independence' in the European Union.

We can leave the last word with John himself:

But there are always 'dominant' cultures that glorify the present order and attribute all social progress to it. It is the duty of socialists to show otherwise. History has a role. The present generation has to possess the knowledge that everything of value was won by struggle against those who sustain injustice, won by real people, by their forebears. It is this that must define our national futures.[16]

Notes

1 J. Foster, 'Scottish Capitalism and the Origins of Nationality', in T. Dickson (ed.), *Scottish Capitalism: Class, State and Nation from before the Union to the Present* (John Donald, Edinburgh: 1982), 19-62.

2 See, for example, Y.V. Bromley, 'The Term Ethnos and its Definition', in *Soviet Anthropology and Ethnography Today – Studies in Anthropology*, Vol. 1 (De Gruyter Mouton, Berlin: 1974), 55-72.

3 J. Foster, 'The Origins of Scottish Nationhood', *Historical Materialism*, 10, 1 (2002), 270.

4 *Manifesto of the Communist Party* (Lawrence & Wishart, London: 1983), 48.

5 *Manifesto of the Communist Party*, 48.

6 J. Foster, *Nations and Working Class Unity in Britain* (Communist Party of Britain, Croydon: 2023), 9.

7 V.I. Lenin, 'Critical Remarks on the National Question', *Collected Works*, Vol. 20 (Progress Publishers, Moscow: 1972), 17-51.

8 V.I. Lenin, 'The National Pride of the Great Russians', *Collected Works*, Vol. 21 (Progress Publishers, Moscow: 1974), 102-6.

9 V.I Lenin, 'The Revolutionary Proletariat and the Right of Nations to Self-Determination', in *Collected Works*, Vol. 21 (Progress Publishers, Moscow: 1974), 407-14.

10 'Marxism and the National Question', reprinted in J.V Stalin, *Marxism and the National and Colonial Question* (Lawrence & Wishart, London: 1936), 8.

11 Foster, 'Origins of Scottish Nationhood', 265.

12 Foster, *Nations and Working Class Unity*, 12.

13 H. Pollitt, *Dimitrov Accuses the Nazis* (Communist Party of Great Britain, London: 1941), 8.

14 G. Dimitrov, *Selected Works*, Vol. 2 (Sofia Press, Sofia, 1972), 86-119.

15 Dimitrov, *Selected Works*, Vol 2, 86-119.

16 Foster, *Nations and Working Class Unity*, 47.

5 PAULINE BRYAN

The Red Paper on Scotland: tracing Scottish capitalism and anti-capitalist resistance

Introduction

JOHN FOSTER has been a constant presence in Scottish politics for over half a century. He was an important influence on the seminal publication, *The Red Paper on Scotland* which was written in 1975 when Harold Wilson was Prime Minister and is still referenced today.[1] This chapter will trace his contribution to Red Paper publications over a period of nearly fifty years.

In 2005, a second *Red Paper on Scotland* appeared edited by Vince Mills, a leading activist in the Campaign for Socialism.[2] This marked the 30th anniversary of the original and explored how the Blair/Brown years had shifted the Labour Party to a firmly neoliberal economic approach. It was published six years after the Scottish Parliament had been established, a Parliament which was already a disappointment to many who had campaigned for its introduction. For them, Scottish Labour had failed to use the powers the Parliament offered to deliver a significant shift in the balance of wealth and power in Scotland. Just two years later, the Scottish National Party would go on to win power and hold it until the present day.

When the nationalists won a second term in 2011 with an overall majority of seats in the Parliament, a referendum on independence was almost inevitable. The Red Paper Collective, which included some of the contributors to the 2005 book, was established at the very end of the year to explore the issues relating to devolution and independence. It published magazines, pamphlets and in 2013 a third book, *Class, Nation and Socialism: The Red Paper on Scotland 2014*, edited by Pauline Bryan and Tommy Kane. It included a joint essay from John Foster, who had by then contributed to all three volumes, alongside MSPs, trade unionists, academics and political activists.[3]

The need for democratic control of the Scottish economy

John Foster's contribution to the original *Red Paper* traced the history of Scotland's politics and economics over centuries. The same forces which shaped Scotland's capitalism also created the forces of anti-capitalist resistance, central to the events surrounding publication in 1975.

The opening paragraph of this volume, written by its editor, the 24-year-old

Gordon Brown, reads:

> The irresistible march of recent events places Scotland today at a turning point – not of our own choosing but where a choice must sooner or later be made. A resurgent nationalism which forces on to the agenda the most significant constitutional decisions since the Act of Union is one aspect of what even the *Financial Times* has described as 'a revolt of rising expectations.' But the proliferation of industrial unrest and the less publicised mushrooming of community action also bears witness to the sheer enormity of the gap now growing between people's conditions of living and their legitimate aspirations.[4]

Brown goes on to ask:

> How can we harness our material resources and social energies to meet the needs of five million people and more? What social structure can guarantee to people the maximum control and self-management over the decisions which affect their lives, allowing the planned co-ordination of the use and distribution of resources, in a co-operative community of equals?[5]

For nearly five decades, John Foster has continued to address these same questions. His 1975 essay had the title 'Capitalism and the Scottish Nation'. His position was that 'unless we understand Scotland's overall relation to capitalism, we cannot define either our attitude to Scotland as nation or Britain as a state.'[6]

In tracing Scotland's history from pre-feudalism to the 1707 Act of Union, he argues that Scotland established a non-colonial political relationship with England, quite different from that of Ireland and the American colonies. This did not mean that it was an 'equal union'.

Scottish industry had experienced disadvantages, but this did not result in demands for home rule or independence. Foster considers that the most plausible explanation for this is that Scottish industry was geared to production for Britain's empire. This had benefits, but there was a price, and that came after the First World War with the decimation of ship building and steel production. Scotland failed to develop the new industries that were emerging in electrical engineering, petrochemicals and cars. Instead, investment flooded to the southeast of England.

That pattern persists to this day, with the continued decline of Scottish-owned manufacturing. From a Marxist standpoint, Foster argued that the culture or institutions of a nation are not absolute or static but reflect and record the changing class conditions. He cited the Scottish Trade Union Council's (STUC) approach in the early 1970s:

> In a period when the manipulation of intra-British national differentials is part

and parcel of monopoly capitalist exploitation it remains a paramount need for all workers in Britain to ensure that the Welsh and Scottish people secure control of their own economies: that the establishment of national parliaments becomes part of the overall struggle against monopoly capitalism.[7]

Foster's ground-breaking chapter has helped shape Red Paper publications down to the present, as they explore how democratic structures and the economy shape our society and our resistance.

Democratic and undemocratic structures

The Red Paper Collective argues that any constitutional change must be measured against its potential to challenge the power of capitalism and bring the economy under democratic control. The purpose of achieving democratic control is to enable a variety of forms of public ownership, to build a sustainable and secure economy, and to redistribute wealth, both from the rich to the rest of the population, and geographically from areas of greater wealth to areas of need.

At the 1968 STUC Congress, Mick McGahey made a distinction between 'healthy nationalism' and chauvinism and went on to call for a federal arrangement for the UK. Conference reports were more extensive than now, and the account of his speech reads:

> His colleagues and he rejected out-rightly the theory of separating Scotland from a United Kingdom, nor did they accept the theory of a classless Scotland at the present stage. They had more in common with the London dockers, the Durham miners and the Sheffield engineers than they ever had had with the barons and landlord traitors of that kind in Scotland.[8]

McGahey and other trade union leaders had a significant effect on the analysis put forward by Gordon Brown in his 1975 introduction. Brown may now reject his earlier views, but for the Red Paper Collective that analysis still resonates and arguably is more relevant now than ever. Particularly, when he suggested that:

> The social and economic problems confronting Scotland arise not from national suppression nor from London mismanagement (although we have had our share of both) but from the uneven and uncontrolled development of capitalism and the failure of successive governments to challenge and transform it. Thus, we cannot hope to resolve such problems merely by recovering a lost independence or through inserting another tier of government: what is required is planned control of our economy and transformation of democracy at all levels.[9]

As the third *Red Paper* noted in 2013:

The only form of constitutional change offered in the referendum is not what was traditionally demanded by the Scottish trade union and labour movement. What is on offer in this referendum would break the class unity of working people across the nations of Britain without breaking the chains of economic control that bind them.[10]

This analysis led the Red Paper Collective to promote progressive federalism. From memory, it was John Foster who coined the term 'progressive federalism', certainly in the Red Paper Collective discussions. He recognised the need to assess where specific powers should be exercised, arguing for 'a significant level of needs-based income redistribution at a federal level combined with maximum scope for the development of economic democracy at national level.'[11]

Foster was acutely conscious that 'devolution' could be used to dilute rather than enhance democratic control. After the independence referendum, the Tories began to address devolution in England including the extension of Metro Mayors. Foster wrote that the Cities and Local Government Act (2016):

...provides institutional structures designed to *demobilise* democratic, pro-people movement for progressive change and *maximise* those of corporate power. Progressive federalism seeks to do the reverse: to create a legal framework that, in terms of economic policy, assists the mobilisation of democratic, pro-people forces – in the knowledge that while legal frameworks can assist progressive outcomes, ultimately these will depend on the political strength of the working-class movement and its allies at both national and federal levels.[12]

The Scottish economy

Foster remained focussed on tracing how Scotland's place within Britain was central to the development of its economy. For the 30th anniversary of the first Red Paper in 2005, his contribution, 'Scotland's Energy Crisis', identified a problem that had spanned the decades between the two volumes.[13] The 1975 *Red Paper* appeared following the first global oil crisis and the successful miners' strikes of the 1970s. The Labour Government had come into power with a radical manifesto commitment to 'an irreversible shift in the balance of power and wealth in favour of working people'. Oil, gas and coal were to be at the heart of British and Scottish politics.

Foster starts his essay in the second *Red Paper* with the prescient statement that: 'For most people Scotland's energy crisis is not immediate. But urgent action is needed now if Scotland is to avoid a severely disabling crisis in the longer term.'[14] He identified that energy policy is not simply a technical matter. It is central to the politics of our time. Writing in the aftermath of the invasions of Afghanistan in 2001 and Iraq in 2003, he argues changes of policy invariably involve struggles over resources between rich and poor nations and rich and poor people. This observation has been reinforced in the twenty years since it was written.

The struggle for the control of energy has seen political interventions at home and military interventions abroad. Speaking for the Labour Government in 2003, Patricia Hewitt argued that 'securing reliable energy supplies will need to be an increasingly important part of a European and foreign policy'.[15] As Foster writes: 'The dirty reality of this policy can be followed daily in Iraq and Afghanistan – as can the omens for its success.'[16]

Scottish energy companies were investing externally rather than at home. They had two thirds of their investment outside Scotland, increasingly in the USA. British energy companies were being bought up by better-resourced and more productive German and French companies – often partly state-owned. The UK and Scottish governments had diminishing ownership or control of vital energy provision.

Foster predicted that: 'Prices could easily double or treble in real terms. An increasing number of people and industries will find themselves priced out of the market.'[17] He goes on to consider solutions including systematically reducing energy consumption, producing sustainable energy and ensuring the full recovery and best use of remaining indigenous fossil fuels. Again, two decades later, these issues remain a major focus for the left.

The external ownership of energy resources in Scotland reflected what was happening across the whole economy. In the third *Red Paper* in 2013, Foster, with Richard Leonard, provided a wide-ranging review exposing the erosion of Scotland's productive base, its lack of long-term investment and the very real danger that 'within two decades its remaining areas of productive strength will have been lost.'[18] They further consider the dramatic shift in ownership away from Scotland; key decisions are increasingly geared to profit targets enforced by externally based investors, resulting in lack of investment and closures.

Under both Labour and the SNP, Scotland had no industrial strategy for indigenous growth, aiming instead to attract overseas investment. The result was the takeover of Scotland's few remaining independent companies and the extraction of profit to the detriment of investment, resulting in job loss and impoverished communities.

Anti-capitalist resistance

When writing in the third *Red Paper*, Foster reflected on the industrial strength of the trade unions in the 1970s:

> Forty years ago industrial closures were successfully resisted. In the most
> celebrated instance, when eight thousand shipbuilding workers had

occupied their yards on the Upper Clyde, Edward Heath's Conservative Government was compelled to reverse its plans and instead to embark on an active programme of regional investment. In achieving this result, the Work-In itself was the crucial lever. But it was a lever that was deployed strategically. It was used by the stewards and the Scottish Trades Union Congress… to develop a broader alliance, principally with small and medium business, which broke the then dominant grip of the Conservative Party in Scottish politics. Its success depended in large measure on an understanding of the conflicts of interest that existed within Scottish capital.[19]

Between the first and second *Red Papers*, Scotland had experienced Thatcherism and the adoption of the same neoliberal policies by Blair and Brown. Thatcher set out to curb the powers of the trade unions and criminalise their legitimate actions. Blair did little to reverse the worst aspects of the Thatcher years, giving way to pressure from the CBI and other business interests.

Across all his contributions, John Foster has consistently supported both political mobilisation at a British level, while developing accountable and democratic ownership at the Scottish level. He argued that the Scottish Parliament needed powers: to provide state aid to strategic and socially essential industries; to develop various forms of public, democratic ownership and taxation, and to borrow on a scale that matches these responsibilities. He concluded that: 'Winning these objectives would begin to lay the foundations for the political economy of social progress'.[20]

He poses the question as to whether there can be a similar alliance across Scotland between politicians, trade unionists and small business, united by concerns about regional policy and deindustrialisation that played a major part in building the demand for a Scottish Parliament.

In further important article written for the Red Paper Collective in 2015 John Foster and Alan Mackinnon asked, 'Why Class Politics?':

Can working people more easily and, in terms of class objectives more effectively, organise themselves at Scottish level or at British level? Do the structures provided by the trade union movement still offer the best vehicle or do new organisations have to be formed that, in current circumstances, harness feelings of national identity? Even more sharply, are class politics still feasible at British level or have the traditional organisations for working class mobilisation already been irretrievably compromised?[21]

The answer was that class resistance had to be mobilised at *both* Scottish and British levels and that the trade union movement still had to be at its heart

– though strengthened by broader political and social movements. They gave three reasons. First, the ownership of Scotland's productive resources lies overwhelmingly outside Scotland, principally at British level. Secondly, the state power which defends this ownership is deployed at British level. The third reason relates to the fallibility of national identity. Any political mobilisation based on national identity only remains progressive and able to reflect the aspirations and interests of the working people in so far as it is sustained by, and linked to, a movement with clear class objectives and which explicitly challenges the power of capital.

That is why John Foster, and the Red Paper Collective, continue to insist that: 'a joint struggle on class terms, uniting working people across the nations of Britain, provides the only realistic basis for Left advance and for maintaining the radical, socialist content of the Scottish identity'.[22]

Notes

1   J. Foster, 'Capitalism and the Scottish Nation', in G. Brown (ed.), *The Red Paper on Scotland* (Edinburgh University Students' Publication Board, Edinburgh: 1975), 141-152.
2   V. Mills (ed.), *The Red Paper on Scotland* (Research Collecttions @ Glasgow Caledonian University, Glasgow: 2005).
3   (With R. Leonard), 'What's Wrong with Scotland's Economy?', in P. Bryan, and T. Kane (eds), *Class, Nation and Socialism: The Red Paper on Scotland 2014* (Glasgow Caledonian University Archives, Glasgow: 2013).
4   Brown, *Red Paper*, 7.
5   Brown, *Red Paper*, 7.
6   Foster, 'Capitalism', 141.
7   Foster, 'Capitalism', 150.
8   STUC Congress Report 1968, Records of the Scottish Trades Union Congress, Glasgow Caledonian University Archives and Special Collections.
9   Brown, *Red Paper*, 7.
10 Bryan and Kane, *Red Paper 2014*, 4.
11 J. Foster, E. Gibbs, and R. Leonard, 'Federalism, the Scottish Economy and Economic Democracy', in *Progressive Federalism* (Red Paper Collective, Glasgow· 2016), 8-11.
12 Foster, 'Federalism', 8.
13 J. Foster, 'Scotland's Energy Crisis', in V. Mills (ed.), *The Red Paper on Scotland* (Research Collections @ Glasgow Caledonian University, Glasgow: 2005), 37-54.
14 Foster, 'Energy Crisis', 37.
15 *Energy White Paper*, House of Commons Debates, 24 February 2003, Vol. 400, cc.26-44.
16 Foster, 'Energy Crisis', 43.
17 Foster, 'Energy Crisis', 48.
18 J. Foster and R. Leonard, 'Introduction (Economy)', in Bryan and Kane, *Class, Nation and Socialism*, 10.
19 'Economic Policy, Class Alliance and Political Influence in Scotland', 22.
20 Foster and Leonard, 'Introduction', 11.
21 J. Foster and A Mackinnon, 'Why Class Politics?', in P. Bryan (ed.), *Scotland: Myths, Realities and Radical Future* (Red Paper Collective, Glasgow: 2015), 15.
22 Foster and Mackinnon, 'Class Politics?', 19.

6 MARJORIE MAYO
AND SUSAN GALLOWAY

Communists in the community

Introduction

JOHN FOSTER'S exceptional work, as a Marxist theoretician and as a Marxist educationalist and activist, provides the starting point for this chapter, focussing on his particular impact as a communist in the community. These examples demonstrate the potential significance of such struggles. With effective political leadership, community activism can address people's immediate needs *and* facilitate the development of class consciousness for the longer-term. Having illustrated the importance of these community-based contributions, both in theory and in practice, the chapter concludes by reflecting on some possible implications for the development of class consciousness through community struggles in the coming period.

The significance of community-based class struggles

John Foster has made outstanding contributions to historical materialist understandings of class formation and class consciousness, through workers' experiences of class struggle – the movement from 'class of itself' to 'class for itself'. Quoting Marx, he has explained that: 'It was... workers' collective defence of their wages and conditions that constituted the working class as a class "of itself". It then became progressively, through struggle and confrontation with capitalist state power, a class "for itself" with an understanding of the need to overthrow that state power'.[1] Trade unions have been central to the development of class consciousness, as Marx so clearly demonstrated. But trade unions have not been the only conduit for its development. On the contrary, class struggles in the community have also been – and continue to be – significant.

Definitions of 'communities' have been contested, with shifting meanings over time.[2] The term is often used to refer to 'communities of identity' in the contemporary context, reflecting current concerns with the politics of identity, along with the politics of resistance to selective forms of discrimination and oppression. Whilst these dimensions of community struggles have continuing significance, this chapter is specifically focused on the more widespread use of the term – 'communities of locality' – communities based around shared geographical spaces.

In the past, working-class communities have been based around just such shared spaces, located around traditional industries, such as shipbuilding, as in Govan, Glasgow. These areas have generally had long histories of community-based struggles, often, although not always, linked to the workplaces in question. These struggles have varied from place to place, over time, with uneven progress in the formation of class consciousness as a result.

In addition to workplace struggles, communities have a history of coming together to act around the issues that concern them in their neighbourhoods too, such as the lack of decent affordable housing. But the capitalist state will not necessarily provide the services that working-class communities need, let alone provide public services in empowering ways. In fact, the capitalist state typically responds only when there is sufficient pressure from below – and when this can be achieved without upsetting the operations of the private market. Which brings communities right up against the capitalist state, in struggle.

Historical examples of such struggles include the Glasgow rent strike during the First World War, based on women's struggles in their communities – community-based struggles that were backed by workers in the munitions industry, threatening strike action in their support. These struggles went beyond the immediate issue of rent rises too, going on to demand council housing and state controls on the housing market. Such demands challenge the role of the capitalist state and the potential for developing socialised – rather than market-dominated – provision, raising class consciousness about the need for transformative futures in the process. John Foster's own historical writings on the formation of class and the development of class consciousness provide important ways into developing understandings of precisely such connections, along with the importance of political leadership.[3]

In addition to his theoretical output, Foster's contributions as an activist in the community demonstrate the significance of such communist leadership in practice. As Jonathan White argues, communists provide leadership to the working-class movement when they embody the general interests of the class, laying out the line of march for the class as a whole, based on an understanding of the conditions driving history.[4] White goes on to cite the *Manifesto of the Communist Party's* description of communists as 'the most advanced and resolute section' of the working class, understanding not just the immediate balance of forces but also the underlying forces at work, thus enabling them to identify the next key step ahead. This is precisely how John Foster has provided leadership in local community struggles. His contributions as a leading activist in Govan illustrate precisely how and why such struggles have been so important, and continue to be so important, both in theory and in practice.

Community action and class consciousness: John Foster's outstanding contributions in Govan.

When John analysed the material basis for class consciousness displayed in the work-in at Upper Clyde Shipbuilders (UCS) in 1971-72, he was writing about events that had taken place just prior to his arrival as a Govan resident.[5] UCS was a battle for economic democracy and for jobs, but also for the future of a community then undergoing rapid change. Comprehensive Redevelopment was reducing Govan's population from a peak of 100,000 to 27,000 today.[6] A local campaign to save and refurbish tenements led to the formation of Scotland's first community-based housing association in 1971.[7] John became a tenant.

In the 50 years since then, John has dedicated his time to building and maintaining the community organisations essential for the defence and advancement of working-class interests, principally the Govan Community Council (GCC) and the Central Govan Tenants Association. Strong links were maintained between the GCC and workplace trade unionism in the Govan shipyard and at other local employers. John served as an officer of GCC, always with the emphasis on action.[8] As part of the GCC collective, he was an organiser, writer (of leaflets, press releases and the Community Council newsletter) and active street campaigner. Over the half century of John's involvement, GCC was at the forefront of scores of campaigns, often in alliance with East Govan or all four 'G51' Community Councils. The following section briefly summarises these, before focusing on the anti-Poll Tax campaign in Govan.

GCC: an overview

Over the past 50 years, GCC has taken the state on at local and national levels to get the public services and amenities to which local people have a right.[9] It has also fought for working-class interests in relation to strategic public planning decisions, where these affect the long-term future of the community. In so doing it has worked closely with its local and national elected representatives whilst also holding them, and public servants, to account.

In the 1990s, for instance, community-led inquiries were initiated by GCC into the effects of Compulsory Competitive Tendering on local hospital services, and into provision for young people and lone parents. GCC set up broad community campaigns to oppose water privatisation, housing stock transfer, and later the Bedroom Tax, the latter involving the local MP, housing associations and the Govan Law Centre, established in 1994. Housing and social problems were continuous concerns. GCC's newsletter was used to share advice on housing and social security matters and to publicise the help provided by local organisations. In summary then, GCC took on, and often pursued to a national level, strategic environmental, housing and employment matters affecting local people, often assisted by the Law Centre.[10]

In addition, since 2000-01 hundreds of asylum seekers have been settled in Govan through the UK Government's 'dispersal' programme. The support given by GCC, including that provided through John's help with casework, drew on the area's 200-year history in relation to immigration, building upon its record of work in the 1980s and 1990s, and bringing organisations and services together to tackle manifestations of racism and hate crime.[11]

In 2002, the GCC also initiated a Public Petition on the Future of Govan which was heard by the Scottish Parliament's Public Petitions Committee two years later. In 1995, the four G51 Community Councils had already produced their own Regeneration Plan for Greater Govan based on community consultation.[12] The Petition was motivated by concerns about the City Plan for Govan, made in contrast, over the heads of the community and at its expense.[13] The Central Govan Action Plan 2006-2022 which followed set out to bring £120 million investment to regenerate central Govan, attracting new residents and creating jobs. To this has been added City Region Deal money to fund a new bridge between Govan and Partick. Despite all this, however, alongside the physical redevelopment of Govan, public services continue to be savaged and destitution is still rising.

Govan against the poll tax (1987 – 1991)

'We will force them to fight us street by street. *We will resist till the tax is scrapped.'*[14] Marx and Engels wrote that the alteration of consciousness can only take place in a 'practical moment'; in other words, it is only in the process of practical struggle, through collective action, that the contradictions and class nature of the current system are revealed.[15]

The anti-Poll Tax campaign provided, without doubt, just such a local 'practical moment', perhaps the first in local community politics since the UCS occupation. The process of mass resistance that defeated this tax was a moment when the class nature of the system was revealed and class consciousness raised, including amongst sections of the population with no previous interest in formal 'politics'. The potential for this was recognised early in Govan. In John's words, 'they are hurting the poor to buy the votes of the better off.'[16] 'This is why the Poll Tax represents such a great political challenge', he later explained: 'It affects everyone. It is an issue that could unite, in active struggle, virtually every section of the population.'[17] These ideas found popular expression in the language and tactics of the local campaign, with a mass burning of Poll Tax demand forms at Govan Cross in April 1989, timed to coincide with the Poll Tax coming into force in Scotland, 'in solidarity with those who will be penalised so harshly because they simply cannot afford to pay.[18] In October 1989, the people of Govan were invited to 'Bury Thatcher under a mass non-payment drive' by signing a pledge of non-payment and sticking it on a huge cartoon poster of the Tory Prime Minister.

The strength of local opposition to the tax and antipathy towards the official Labour Party position were important factors in the Govan by-election in November 1988, when the Scottish National Party (SNP) overturned a Labour majority of 19,000.

Together, the four Greater Govan Community Councils formed 'Govan Against the Poll Tax' (GAPT) in the autumn of 1987 with the aim of forcing the government to abandon the Poll Tax by making it unworkable. It had the support of the local tenants' associations and the shipyard shop stewards. There were several stages to this Govan campaign between 1987 and 1991, which initially focused on non-registration (1987-88), then non-payment (1989-90), and then on the defence of those who could not or would not pay – through mass mobilisations to prevent 'poindings' and warrant sales, and through petitioning to prevent arrestment of wages (1990-91).[19]

The approach in Govan had several hallmarks. First, priority was given at each stage to maximising and unifying opposition to the tax by finding ways for every individual and household to take part, based on their own circumstances, while organising practical solidarity for those who could not afford to pay. Secondly, street-by-street organising was crucial, drawing upon the tradition of the First World War rent strikes. This was the bedrock of the Govan campaign throughout. It began with the canvassing of thousands of individual households in the district, urging people not to register and collecting pledges not to do so. Householders were urged to hand over their registration forms and to put 'no registration' posters in their windows. This approach was followed through at each stage, helping to persuade and to 'test the temperature'. The front page of the GCC 'Govan Letter' of May-June 1991 displays two memorable images of the very same close, 10 Hutton Drive, Govan, one showing rent strikers defeating an eviction in November 1915, the other showing crowds on 3 May 1991, repelling sheriff officers from attempting a poinding, during the third stage of the campaign.

Another hallmark of GAPT's approach was its non-partisan nature. Both SNP and Labour politicians spoke at its public meetings and GAPT was affiliated to both the Strathclyde Anti-Poll Tax Federation and the Scottish TUC campaign. A final feature was the range of tactics deployed including direct action. In April 1990, a twenty-strong delegation from GCC occupied the offices of a firm of sheriff officers demanding a written statement of reassurance to protect local people, while the first mass action to prevent a poinding in Govan took place in 1991.[20]

The scale of mass resistance and non-payment of the Poll Tax sealed its fate. By early 1990, non-payment in Glasgow was 30 per cent, despite tens of thousands of summary warrants being issued.[21] In some Govan schemes it was as high as 80 per cent.[22] When the Tory Government finally capitulated in March 1991, the lessons of this victory were not lost in Govan. It showed 'the power of ordinary people when united together and convinced of the justice of their case'.[23] The people of Govan had 'played their part in repeating the great victories of 1915 and 1919.'[24]

In his 50 years of continuous community leadership John has demonstrated persistence in keeping local organisations going, resilience in the face of barriers, but always focused on the next step, the next action, upon the possibilities ahead.[25] His clarity of class analysis, belief in Govan's people, and his determination and consistency have never been more necessary.

Communists in the community and the development of class consciousness in the coming period

Working-class communities of locality are currently experiencing major changes. De-industrialisation has seen to that. Industrial jobs have been disappearing. Meanwhile, urban redevelopment schemes have been exacerbating the processes of gentrification, pushing up rents and prices and so squeezing working-class people out of their areas, increasing inequalities and leaving communities more fragmented as a result.[26] There are major challenges for working-class community activism here, although there remain significant possibilities for building alliances. As the evidence from this chapter demonstrates, new opportunities exist to bring people together, united in solidarity around their shared interests and concerns around jobs and services. Neoliberal policies have led to increasing marketisation across the range of public services including housing, education, transport, health and social care. So, whatever their differences, communities have been sharing experiences of coming in direct conflict against the capitalist state.

Communities may have been fragmenting in some ways. Gentrification has been affecting their class composition – that is if class is defined by occupation and skill. However, the Marxist definition of class starts from people's relationships to the means of production, rather than defining them by whether they have manual or non-manual employment. According to Marxists, the working class – the proletariat – is defined as those who sell their labour power, whether they work by hand or by brain. And this includes many of those who would have been defined as 'middle class' in the past, non-manual workers including professionals who are currently experiencing processes of significant change. Precarious employment, with deteriorating pay and conditions and equally precarious housing situations, are becoming more and more widespread (in other words, the processes of proletarianisation in practice).

The scope for developing alliances and building class consciousness would seem to be growing correspondingly, as more and more people face the reality of capitalism. Hence the importance of understanding, and learning from, the contributions of communists in the community – none more so than the exemplary work of John Foster, leading activist as well as leading theoretician.

Notes

1   J. Foster, 'Marx and the British Working Class', *Theory & Struggle*, 121 (2000), 2-9.
2   R. Williams, *Keywords* (Fontana, London 1976), 76.
3   J. Foster, *Class Struggle and the Industrial Revolution: Early Industrial Capitalism in Three English Towns* (Weidenfeld and Nicolson, London: 1974).
4   J. White, *Making Our Own History: A User's Guide to Marx's Historical Materialism* (Praxis Press, Glasgow: 2021), 63.
5   He arrived in winter 1975-76, after moving to Glasgow from Cambridge for academic work in 1968. J. Foster and C. Woolfson, *The Politics of the UCS Work-in: Class Alliances and the Right to Work* (Lawrence and Wishart, London: 1986).
6   F. Crawford, S. Beck and P. Hanlon, *Will Glasgow Flourish?* (Glasgow Centre for Population Health, Glasgow: 2007); City Ward Factsheet, 2017.
7   Central Govan Housing Association, now known as Govan Housing Association. See, R. Young, *Annie's Loo: The Govan Origins of Scotland's Community Based Housing Associations* (Argyll Publishing, Glendaruel: 2013).
8   Danny O'Neill, Chairperson, Govan Community Council (GCC), interview 28 Dec. 2023.
9   GCC has fought for better public transport, local employment and apprenticeships and the defence of local services: Govan Baths and Wash-house, the library and schools, the Job Centre, police and fire services, and, currently, the last bank.
10 An example of a housing issue taken up was a campaign against detrimental changes in government grants for new build housing for social rent. These discriminated against inner-city community-based housing associations, such as those in Govan, *GCC minutes* 12 Jun. 2012.
11 The make-up of the local population has changed with the area's minority ethnic population increasing from 2 per cent to 9 per cent between 2001-2011 and continues to grow.
12 'The Govan Letter', Dec. 1995, John Foster Collection, Glasgow Caledonian University Archives and Special Collections (Foster Collection, GCU Archives).
13 John Foster, GCC, and Mike Dailly, Govan Law Centre, gave evidence to the committee on 23 Jun. 2004.
14 'Central Govan Tenants' Newsletter', Aug.-Dec., Foster Collection, GCU Archives.
15 K. Marx and F. Engels, *The German Ideology* (Progress Publishers, Moscow: 1968). See, J. Foster, 18 May 2023 Marx Memorial Library lecture, 'Class mobilisation and class consciousness: language and the 'practical moment': https://www.marx-memorial-library.org.uk/past-events
16 J. Foster quoted in, 'Stop the tax in its tracks', *Morning Star*, 29 Dec. 1987.
17 J. Foster, 'Mass action can beat the poll tax', *Morning Star*, 8 Oct. 1988.
18 Govan Against the Poll Tax (GAPT) press release, 16 Apr. 1989, Foster Collection, GCU Archives.
19 A 'poinding' is the removal of household goods to recover debts. They were abolished, along with warrant sales, in 2001.
20 'The Govan Letter', Apr./May 1990, Foster Collection, GCU Archives.
21 *Evening Times*, 5 Feb. 1990.
22 'The Govan Letter', Feb./Mar. 1990. GCU Archives, John Foster Collection.
23 GAPT, 'Govan's Anti-Poll Tax News', Apr.-May 1991, Foster Collection, GCU Archives. Although GAPT continued the non-payment campaign to seek a fair settlement, including compensation for local government, an end to warrant sales, an amnesty for non-payers, and a replacement tax based on ability to pay.
24 GAPT, 'Govan's Anti-Poll Tax News', Apr.-May 1991, Foster Collection, GCU Archives.
25 Interview Esme Clark, Secretary GCC, 1 Feb. 2004.
26 D. Dorling, *Peak Inequality* (Policy Press, Bristol: 2018).

Thinking about the British strike wave: class, class struggle and consciousness in 2022-3

JOHN FOSTER'S body of work in labour movement history applies a highly sophisticated historical materialism to the history of the British working class. He uses it to analyse a series of key class struggles and transformations that form the inheritance of the trade union movement in Britain today. In this short essay, I identify some key features of this approach before showing how it can inform the work of a new generation of trade union militants.

The first feature to emphasise is his use of a rigorous materialist dialectics that draws on crucial methodological insights from Marx's *Grundrisse* and developed by Soviet philosopher Evald Ilyenkov, among others. This forms an analytical framework for many of his works, but is explicitly set out in an important essay, 'On Marx's Method and the Study of History'.[1] Central to this methodological approach is an insistence that Marxist analysis entails understanding the way the concepts we use to think about the world arise historically as expressions of material developments and must therefore be defined and used historically, in relation to the wider material developments of which they form part. This is explicitly pitched against neo-Kantian methodologies like structuralism, or so-called Analytical Marxism, for example.

Secondly, I would draw attention to John's close analysis of the specificities of historical change and transitions. For example, he was instrumental in bringing to the attention of English-speaking Marxists the work of Soviet historian Alexander Chistozvonov. In his work Foster sees a methodology that enables close comparative study and deeper understanding of the key factors that must accumulate to drive a qualitative shift – a transition between modes of production. Chistozvonov's approach also helps us to understand why transitions fail to happen in some places and why is it that some ruling classes retain or reassert regulatory control.[2] In a brilliantly thought-provoking article in *Marxism and Struggle*, John further applied his methodology to analysing the issue of the collapse of the Soviet Union.[3]

This brings us to a third related feature, which is the need for rigorous attention to historical concreteness. John's work frequently deploys a comparative approach that enables him to tease out the complexities of uneven material developments that shape the development of often uneven historical consciousness. This is clearly visible in his *Class Struggle and the Industrial Revolution*, but the need to pay close attention to specific and often highly localised features of the material conditions within which humans make their own history runs throughout his work.[4]

Fourth, John's work insists on the importance of Marx's and Lenin's insights into exactly how and when capitalism creates its own gravediggers. Foster's work constantly engages with the interaction of permanently active tendencies with specific conjunctural conditions. Developing insights that are fundamental to *Capital*, he argues that the capitalist mode of production contains within it contradictory tendencies that both reproduce capitalism and create conditions for its possible overthrow. Commodity production and exchange sustain processes of reification and the formation of consumption-based cultures that cut through, stratify and segment the working class. Yet at the same time, the internal dynamics of capitalism constantly generate the potential for class consciousness within the working class, and particularly within specific sections of that class. While the whole working class is subjected to a general process of proletarianisation, there are particular dynamics within large-scale industries that form the basis for the emergence of a wider consciousness of the class nature of society; consolidation into ever larger units of production as capital centralises; increasing subordination of workers to machine technology; the constant revolutionising of the technical base of production as capital seeks to accumulate in competition, together with the rhythms of capitalist crises which lead to the expulsion of living labour from the production process and expose the anarchic character of capitalist competition. These tendencies are located at varying depths of the capitalist mode of production – some are permanently active, others are more complex and historically contingent. To the extent that these operate together, they form a constantly acting tendency that, in certain circumstances, can build the basis for unity, erode the power of reification and lead workers into struggles that can escalate from a consciousness of the struggle over surplus value in a workplace to a wider consciousness of a class interest in systemic change, what Marx called 'class for itself', rather than 'class of itself'.

John's work also shows that this active role of class struggle is a determinant of historical development. The working class is always active in making its own history, in the conditions it inherits from the past, even where that history does not result in a revolutionary transformation of the mode of production. Even where the immediate consequences of struggles appear to be defeats or the ruling class regrouping, one of the most significant elements of John's historical writing is the insistence on analysing what exactly has changed and how these struggles created the conditions for those of the future. For example, in *Class Struggle and the Industrial Revolution,* the struggles of the 1830s in the manufacturing districts contribute toward a change in ruling class strategy that defuses one phase of struggle but crucially lays out the terrain on which future struggles within British capitalism will be waged and creates the forces who will be thrown into those struggles.

Finally, there is his insistence on the importance of Marxists engaging with language. Together with his collaborator Charles Woolfson and influenced by the work of Chik Collins, John Foster has pioneered an approach that gives us tools for examining the way in which struggle is registered and waged within language. This approach is once again explicitly targeted at the rigidities of structuralist and post-structuralist accounts of language, founded as they are on a neo-Kantian philosophy. Where historians like Gareth Stedman Jones drew on these philosophies to present Chartism and class consciousness as linguistic positions, John and his collaborators used the work of Soviet linguistic science to examine how material struggles enter into consciousness through language. Drawing on the work of the Vygotsky school of Leontiev and Luria, as well as Voloshinov, they point toward the importance of seeing language as a social product through which consciousness is mediated, that arises from and reflects contradictory concrete material conditions. In periods of acute class struggle, language can lose its stability and its ability to reproduce the existing order and begin instead to express the collision of material positions. This work also illuminates a linguistic dimension of leadership. Leaders who are embedded in their class, organised and active in its social circles and able to speak with authority can make critical interventions that shift the meaning of words as part of a movement in consciousness.[5]

Above all, John's work, like that of all significant Marxist theorists, provides the working-class movement with an approach that can be a guide to analysis and action. It provides us with ways of understanding the history of our class and the class struggles of the present. Reading John's work helps people involved in contemporary class struggles, particularly in the trade unions to think about the concrete conditions, organisations and actions, practical and linguistic, through which spontaneously arising class struggles can be transformed and develop into a wider class consciousness.

In a recent lecture at the Marx Memorial Library, I attempted to use elements of this approach to venture some preliminary thoughts about the British strike wave of 2022-23.[6] The first, obvious, observation to make about the strike wave was that in no way was this a revolutionary situation. The ruling class in Britain – the finance capitalists and monopolists whose interests predominate in the state apparatus – maintained control in this period. They were, and are, deeply divided and strategically adrift in ways that it is vital for the working-class movement to understand, but equally they were able to continue ruling in the old way. Making any assessment of how the ruling class organised in the state apparatus viewed the strike wave is difficult not least because internal papers documenting the government's response are not available for analysis.

However, there were, I believe, germinal signs of a weakening of some of the mechanisms of control. There is evidence that the government attempted to mobilise its allies in the mass media to drive wedges through the strikes, pitching different strata against each other, public and private, using well-worn speech acts. Yet the evidence during the strike wave itself suggests that this failed to resonate – there was no detectable widespread hostility to the strikers – differences in degrees of support perhaps but little more than that and nothing that could be mobilised against them.

To account for this, we need to understand the concrete features of the conjunctural or practical moment. In particular, we need to see the way that the actions of British-based finance and monopoly capital through the state have led to a long-term weakening of established consumer identities, aggravated and compounded in 2022 by a disastrous collapse in living standards. British capitalism, as is widely understood, has been gravely weakened by its peculiar features, most notably the domination of finance capital within its ruling class. Its unusually precipitous deindustrialisation, its dependence on service industries, its weak productivity, low wages and the indebtedness of its working class, all arise from and interact with the power of finance capital over state policy and capitalist investment patterns. The response to the financial crash saw this power expressed once again in the form of massive interventions to support finance capital paid for through a new wave of public spending cuts, austerity and capital scrapping. The consequences of this were manifold but two of significance were the retreat of public spending from deindustrialised regions in the English north and midlands, coupled with a long-term erosion of the material basis of 'middle-class' consumer identities, established from the late 1980s. Access to cheap credit, home ownership, university and decent jobs in the large urban centres was thrown into question. Ideologically, this was registered in anxieties about the fate and actions of people in the 'left behind' deindustrialised zones, and in a series of 'middle-class' anxieties turning on whether the next generation could even reproduce current standards of living.

These longer-term trends were turned into an acute conjunctural crisis for workers by the disastrous collapse in living standards from 2021 onwards as economies opened up in the wake of the Covid-19 pandemic. Monopolies in primary commodities, food and logistics exploited their positions in the context of a demand surge, articulated through fragile supply chains to ramp up prices. Monopolies in the wider capitalist class responded to input price pressures by raising prices and attacking labour costs. In Britain, this was registered in a wave of 'fire and rehire' and driving down of terms and conditions, most notoriously at P&O and British Gas, but experienced particularly keenly in the non-unionised precarious work sectors. As inflation took off in 2022, Central Banks weighed in to compound the pressures on working people by following the finance capital mandate to the letter – driving up interest rates to choke off economic activity and defend the value of financial assets. Workers saw the long-term stagnation in wages compounded by a sharp cut in their value, reinforced by new pressures on mortgage debt and rents.

For the trade union movement, this was a critical test. Where it was organised, there was pressure to respond and an opportunity to demonstrate its utility. The result was a wave of strike action on a scale not seen since the 1980s. Almost always, ballot thresholds for legal industrial action, which had been a significant obstacle in previous years, were exceeded, often with significant margins. Measured in terms of the wage increases won, the results were modest, while cushioning the impact of the cost-of-living crisis for many workers. But to what extent was there, within this strike wave, a deeper mobilisation of the class and any shift in its consciousness?

The trade union movement is, of course, only a partial expression of the British working class as a whole. It is heavily concentrated in the public sector and weakly organised in the extensive retailing sector, for example. Equally, the large-scale manufacturing and primary commodity extraction industries in which the dynamics that Marx, Engels and Lenin identified as forming the basis for potentially mobilising a deeper class consciousness have been severely depleted. Perhaps reflecting this, it is significant that the strike wave was concentrated heavily in Britain's critical national infrastructure. Strike days, for example, were centred on the transport, logistics, storage, information and communication sectors. These tend to be large scale employers in the monopoly sector in which there is particularly strong drive to cut labour costs and impose further automation, together with sharp struggles over the frontier of control within the workplace. While the strike day data reflects in large part the CWU's long-running dispute at Royal Mail and the RMT's and ASLEF's national rail strikes, it is also likely that the majority of Unite's strike days were taken here, as it targeted logistics firms and bus operators. The other main sectors were the public sector education and health strikes, where unions were fighting the government's pay cap. The state was entangled in all these actions. The government imposed the pay cap on public sector workers and mandated pay offers, bankrolled the employers and directed disputes in the rail sector. Beyond this, the Bank of England, which had already turfed out one Tory administration, weighed in regularly to voice finance capital's insistence on the importance of wage restraint. All the while, corporate profits were soaring. In summary, the conjuncture was one in which many of the conditions were present not only for a mobilisation within the class but for a development of consciousness within it. Did this happen? To some extent, it did.

The general proletarianisation processes, compounded by the cost-of-living crisis, appear to have produced some general sense that working people shared a class position. The British Social Attitudes Survey, for example, has registered notable upticks in the last two years in the proportion of people who believe that they are in the working class, that this determines their life chances and that working people do not get a fair share of the nation's wealth. Opinion polls throughout the strike wave showed that most people blamed the government for most of the strikes, while supporting the strikers who had often been 'keyworkers' during the pandemic. Within the striking unions, the utterances of the official labour movement remained, for the most part, firmly within the orbit of trade union ideology. 'We Demand Better', after all, was the theme of the TUC's demonstration in June 2022. Yet on the left of the movement there was a determined and articulate attempt to explain the strike wave as an episode in a class struggle. The RMT's leadership particularly used every platform, internal and external, to express this message. In speeches to mass meetings of strikers, in the new channels of social media within and beyond the labour movement, and in broadcast and print media, a consistent message was used that the strike wave was a class response to a class attack. At the 18 June TUC demonstration in London, RMT general secretary Mick Lynch told the crowd: 'We are on strike in a class struggle now. If your conditions are being attacked, if your pay is being attacked, if your jobs are being stripped from you, you are in a class struggle.' Similarly, on 1 February 2023, he addressed the mass strike rally in London and told the crowd they were part of a reborn, active, struggling class movement: 'Every worker needs a pay rise, every worker needs a square deal. We will not be divided. We are the working class, and we are back.'

This was coupled with robust attacks on corporate profiteering and the vast inequality in wealth. The widespread popularity of this language, measurable in their huge circulation on social media, was significant in itself and provides some echo of the interventions of the Upper Clyde Shipbuilders shop stewards in 1971-72, analysed by John Foster and Charles Woolfson. Class-conscious industrial militants were able to develop a level of leadership and moral authority within the trade union movement and the wider working class. They were able to do this because of their ability to understand the character of the 'practical moment', combined with their rootedness in immediate workplace struggles. In this way, they were able, through language, to give expression to the collision of material positions in a way that sought to bridge the gap between immediate demands and the need to develop consciousness among sections of a class thrown into active struggle. The strikes were thus rearticulated for many people who participated in them, as part of a class-based revolt against an increasingly harsh reality.

The strike wave has inevitably ebbed and it remains to be seen what the lasting legacy will be. It is too early to assess whether the ruling class will have to make a major change 'in front and speech', as Marx would put it, on the scale of the 1840s, or 1919-20, or the strike wave of 1968-74. Yet in the escalating racism of the Tory party and the ruling class consensus over the need for imperialist bellicosity, supported by increased arms spending, the strike wave will have been a factor. For Marxists, there are also key lessons to be learned for organisation within the class: about understanding the conditions under which class consciousness can emerge; about the importance of patient organisation within the class; of the need for constant analysis of the precise character of the practical moment and a recognition of the critical role of language in the exercise of leadership at key moments. The extraordinary body of work that John Foster has produced is an enduring guide for labour movement militants.

Notes

1   j. Foster, 'On Marx's Method and the Study of History', *Theory & Struggle*, 116 (2016), 52-59.
2   A.N. Chistozvonov, 'The Concept and Criteria of Reversibility and Irreversibility of a Historical Process' reproduced in *Our History*, 63 (Summer 1975), 3-11.
3   J. Foster, 'The end of history and historical materialism: A defence of Marxist dialectics', in M. Davis and M. Mayo (eds) *Marxism and Struggle: Toward the Millennium* (Praxis Press, London: 1998), 29-54.
4   J. Foster, *Class Struggle and the Industrial Revolution: Early Industrial Capitalism in Three English Towns* (Weidenfeld and Nicolson, London: 1974).
5   This is well demonstrated in J. Foster and C. Woolfson, *The Politics of the UCS Work-In: Class Alliances and the Right to Work* (Lawrence and Wishart, London: 1986). Also, in his most recent study of class and class consciousness, *Languages of Class Struggle: Communication and Mass Mobilisation in Britain and Ireland 1842-1972* (Praxis Press, Glasgow: 2024).
6   The following argument is set out in more detail in my article, 'Class mobilisation and class consciousness in the British strike wave of 2022-23', *Theory & Struggle*, 125 (2024), 80-8.

Hyper-imperialism today

IN 1990, the Indian Marxist Prabhat Patnaik published an essay in *Monthly Review* called 'Whatever Has Happened to Imperialism?'.[1] The essence of his article was that on both sides of the North Atlantic, the word 'imperialism' had vanished and the theory of imperialism as the structuring principle of the world order had equally been dismissed. The Berlin Wall had fallen and soon the Soviet Union would collapse. This put Marxist writers on the defensive and allowed liberal scholars to argue that the Marxist method was obsolete and that terms such as imperialism had no room in contemporary scholarship. Post-structuralism and post-modernism, both with longer histories of their own rooted in debates in the French academy, advanced the idea that structuring forms such as imperialism and neo-colonialism simply would not stand scrutiny and that scholars had to attend to the complexities of the world order rather than its structures. Use of such terms as imperialism was put down to nostalgia. Marxism is over, we were told, and so with it would go its main concepts.

Prabhat Patnaik's exasperation was not isolated. Many other Marxist scholars felt the same way, and many tried in their different ways to respond to this assault within the academies of North America and Europe. Two edited texts appeared in the 1990s to stake a claim against this attempted evisceration of Marxism. First, from New York in 1997, came a book edited by Ellen Meiksins Wood and John Bellamy Foster called *In Defense of History: Marxism and the Postmodern Agenda* (based on an issue of *Monthly Review* the previous year). That volume contained a spirited defence of Marxism by the US academic Fredric Jameson called 'Five Theses on Actually Existing Marxism'.[2] In that essay, Jameson wrote that Marxism is the 'science of the inherent contradictions of capitalism', which means that as long as capitalism remains intact, Marxism remains its scientific critique. In the same vein, as long as imperialism remains in place, Marxism's theory of it remains necessary. Second, from London in 1998, came a collection edited by Mary Davis and Marjorie Mayo called *Marxism and Struggle: Toward the Millennium*. That work contained an essay by John Foster called 'The end of history and historical materialism: A defence of Marxist dialectics'.[3] The themes in Foster's essay complemented the work that had just come out from *Monthly Review*. Indeed, his essay made the same broad argument as Jameson that Marxism is the necessary scientific critique of capitalism. In the midst of this analysis, both authors defended the idea that imperialism remained a social force in the world and that the Marxist anti-imperialist critique remained essential.

Around the same time, a number of left academics, including well-known Marxists, began to use the theory of Marxism to dismiss the idea of imperialism. In 1916, Lenin had completed his text *Imperialism*, which had been researched and written to answer the question of why the European powers went to war in 1914. Lenin argued that capitalism generated national monopolies, which then tried to exceed their national boundaries through extra-economic mechanisms facilitated by their own national states; these attempts moved inter-capitalist competition into inter-imperialist rivalries. Lenin was not trying to write a general theory of imperialism, but he was interested in trying to explain the conjuncture. To say that the 1990s was not the same as the 1910s is hardly insightful. It is an error to treat Lenin's text as trans-historical both for those who used it uncritically to explain imperialism in its different periods, and for those who used it to attack Marxism as being inflexible. It was in this kind of false debate that a number of post-Marxists emerged to dismiss the idea of imperialism, using their privilege as former Marxists and their knowledge of Marxism.

The most important figures in this counter-revolutionary move were Antonio Negri and Michael Hardt – whose book *Empire* (2000) appeared just as the United States started a new imperialist thrust in Panama (1989), Afghanistan (2001), and Iraq (2003).[4] A few years after Negri and Hardt, the distinguished Marxist geographer David Harvey published *The New Imperialism* (2003), which – despite its name – argued against the category. In that book, but more in subsequent work, Harvey argued that the altered direction of finance shifted the geography of imperialism: if capital fled the South for the North, then how could the structure of imperialism possibly exist? Negri and Hardt used the debate between Lenin and Karl Kautsky to argue, strangely, that Kautsky's theory of ultra-imperialism (that the bourgeoisie was now global and there was therefore no national question) is closer to Marx's analysis and that therefore a better way to understand the problem was through their category of Empire, or a global project with no centre and no identifiable structures of power. Just as Hardt and Negri tried to draw inspiration from their interpretation of Lenin's work, Harvey argued that surplus transfers had reversed direction and that the centres of growth proved where imperialism might be better located. Both Hardt/Negri and Harvey critiqued Lenin's conjunctural theory by understanding it as a trans-historical theory and then built their own theories that vitiated the necessity to use Marxist categories to understand the actual dynamics of neo-colonial structures.

This is where the tradition rooted in *In Defense of History* and *Marxism and Struggle* comes into use. Both books argued that Marxism is not only an essential mode of analysis of capitalism, but that the concepts of Marxism had to consistently and dialectically be developed as capitalism – a dynamic system – unfolded. Marxism had to root itself in the shifts and consolidations of capitalism and imperialism, and not merely inherit conjunctural analyses in a religious fashion. That is what makes the work of Marxists such as John Foster so important for our time. They not only defended the Marxist analytic through a close historical investigation of both structures and struggles, but they opened up space to analyse the present through dynamic Marxist categories.

Hyper-imperialism

In 2021, John Foster wrote an article, 'Halting Imperialism's Drive to War', which argued the following:

> While the empires of the past are gone, monopoly capitalism continues and today its ability draw super-profits from across the world faces a period of acute crisis. We see around us every indication of a new aggressive phase of military activity led by the United States. In this Britain plays a key subsidiary role while the dominant powers in the European Union pursue their own agendas in Eastern Europe and Africa.[6]

When I read this, and particularly the section on the New Cold War, I thought about how this approach was very close to what we had been developing in Tricontinental: Institute for Social Research and with our partners, Global South Insights. This 'new aggressive phase of military activity', we argued, can best be described as a new phase of hyper-imperialism, which I will attempt to explain in the remainder of this essay.

The countries of the Global North are awash with weapons systems that have the capacity to blow up the world many times over. Not only do the countries in the Global North have armies that are lethal and dangerous, but they are the largest exporters of weapons to the rest of the world, fuelling conflicts that could be settled by diplomacy. The larger the arsenal of weapons, the greater the confidence that they will be the arbiter of disputes – and so, even petty problems that can be resolved by negotiations escalate rapidly into war. And, for the countries of the Global North, the idea of diplomacy itself has been reduced to 'military diplomacy', where the generals push aside the civilians and lead the conversation with braggadocio. It is this overwhelming military power of the Global North that has inaugurated the stage of hyper-imperialism, an imperialism that is dangerous and decadent.

The name hyper-imperialism is chosen to indicate the frenetic character of this imperialism, the over-enthusiastic use of armed force to settle problems. It is a name that suits the attitude of the Global North, which operates as a bloc through a political formation (the G7), a military alliance (NATO), and an intelligence sharing operation (the Fourteen Eyes Intelligence network). The United States is at the core of this hyper-imperialist bloc, with the subordinate allies of Europe, Japan, and South Korea obediently following Washington's whims. It is not enough to provoke a war in Ukraine by pushing NATO eastwards, but the Global North's hyper-imperialist bloc is now poking and prodding in eastern Asia through the attempted expansion of NATO and through provocations regarding Taiwan. It is almost as if the hyper-imperialist bloc desires a massive world war that would be focused on its adversaries, what it considers its 'near-peer rivals' of China and Russia.

One of the notable features of the politics of the Global North countries has been the absolute decline in the intellectual calibre of its leadership. The issue in the United States, for instance, is not merely the age of Joe Biden or the madness of Donald Trump or the shallowness of Kamala Harris. It is, in fact, that neither Biden nor Trump, nor indeed Germany's Scholz or France's Macron have a project for their countries. None of these leaders provide a pathway out of the economic malaise in their countries, a malaise that has been deepened by the lack of productive investment and the inflationary pressure due to the war in Ukraine. Their speeches sound exhausted; their ideas are shop-worn. In fact, the lack of a project is what makes the ruling classes of the Global North decadent.

In the United States, for instance, child poverty more than doubled last year from the year before, and overall poverty rates have increased to decade-long highs (this is the largest one-year increase in poverty ever recorded). Part of this increase is due to the expiration of emergency measures put in place by the Biden administration. But this is not the only reason. There is simply no plan to re-energise the economy in areas forgotten by the ruling class, as factory deserts were shaped by the arbitrage calculations of financiers about forty years ago. The fight in the US Congress is over tax credits to enable the poor to get some income in hand, but nothing more than that. There is no project to end poverty. That makes the ruling class decadent in its worldview. It is out of this decadence that we see the rise of far-right forces.

The peaceful rise of the Global South countries poses a comprehensive economic challenge to imperialist world dominance. For the first time in six hundred years, the Atlantic imperialist powers are confronted with a non-white economic force capable of countering them. The answer of the hyper-imperialist bloc is to move to force, either sanctions or war. The countries that are being threatened by the Global North – particularly China and Russia – are largely defensive powers, with the military means to defend themselves but not to take on the military force of the Global North. China's military spending, for instance, is much smaller than that of the Global North (it is responsible for

10.2 per cent of global military spending, with Russia responsible for 3 per cent and India for 2.8 per cent). The United States spends 21 times more on its military per person than China does on its military – almost 40 per cent of global expenditure on armaments.

It is clear that the Global South, in contrast to the Global North, is not a bloc and certainly not a military bloc. The Global South thus faces the extreme monopoly of military spending by the US-led Military Bloc. This represents a clear and present danger to all countries of the Global South; it presents an imminent danger to the continued existence of humankind and the planet. In turn, the single most important aspect of state power – that is, military power – the absolute central danger to the working classes of *all* countries, especially to the darker nations of the world, lies in the US-led Imperialist camp. Objectively, there is no such thing as sub-imperialism or non-Western imperialist powers (such concepts are subjective deceptions that cloud over the factual realities). There is one imperialism, a hyper-imperialism.

Notes

1   P. Patnaik, 'Whatever Happened to Imperialism', *Monthly Review*, 42, 6 (1990), 1-7.
2   F. Jameson, 'Five Theses on Actually Existing Marxism', in E. Meiksins Wood and J. Bellamy Foster (eds), *In Defense of History: Marxism and the Postmodern Agenda* (Monthly Review Press, New York: 1997), 175-84.
3   J. Foster, 'The end of history and historical materialism: A defence of Marxist dialectics', in M. Davis and M. Mayo (eds) *Marxism and Struggle: Toward the Millennium* (Praxis Press, London: 1998), 29-54.
4   A. Negri and M. Hardt, *Empire* (Harvard University Press, Harvard: 2000).
5   D. Harvey, *The New Imperialism* (Oxford University Press, Oxford: 2003).
6   *Morning Star*, 14 Aug. 2021.

Religion and English radical history

JOHN FOSTER is the foremost historian of the British Marxist tradition today. His scholarship and active involvement in the History Group of the Communist Party of Great Britain (CPGB) makes him a crucial connection between the postwar British Marxist historians (A.L. Morton, Christopher Hill, Dona Torr, Rodney Hilton, Eric Hobsbawm and others) and the Marxist historians represented in this collection. In the Communist Party and the labour movement, he is also known for his work on progressive federalism. Both these areas of interest are, of course, interrelated. British Marxist historians have a strong tradition of studying national and regional histories in order to understand the development of exploitation and resistance and to promote stories of the past that challenge those of the ruling class.

In this short essay, I want to revive part of this tradition that involves religion. Postwar British Marxist historians were pioneers in understanding the role of religion in the transition from feudalism to capitalism and in resistance to capitalism. Odd though religion is to many Marxists and historians today, it must be part of an analysis that uses our national and regional histories to explain exploitation today and how we got to where we are. But it is also an exercise in imagining a transformed world and how this might be brought about.

1381

A convenient starting point for English radical history is the so-called Peasants' Revolt from the summer of 1381. This is typically chosen because it represents a moment where class interests from below were stated as starkly as they had ever been in English feudal history. The arguments for this are uncontroversial. The decades following the Black Death (1348-49) wiped out nearly half the population. The labour shortage provided opportunities for peasants and land workers while the ruling class tried to cap wages, restrict mobility, and keep serfs tied to the land. Taxation for costly wars and lack of protection from coastal attacks had already heightened tensions, but the 1380 poll tax provided a more immediate stimulus to revolt.

It is now common to note that the label 'Peasants' Revolt' does not do justice to the social complexity of the uprising. It is true that, in addition to peasants, there were local officials, artisans, urban dwellers, prisoners, and lower clergy. This partly explains why the uprising was such a widespread and networked phenomenon. But concerns about peasant exploitation remained integral to the grievances: one of the key demands made by Wat Tyler, for instance, was the end of serfdom. From the lower clergy, John Ball gave voice to the exploitation of the peasantry. Ball criticised the lords for their fine clothing, luxurious houses, and good food. He contrasted this with the conditions of those working the fields through wind and rain for the benefit of the lords.[1]

Ball articulated discontent in theological and biblical terms, almost the only language available for him to do so. He looked back to Adam and Eve to argue that this was a time when there were no lords exploiting the peasantry. This largely backward-looking myth was then used to critique the present and point to a new societal order in England. Alongside Ball as the new religious leader would be a 'just king' in the figure of Richard II, minus his corrupt advisors. Rebels like Ball, Tyler and their supporters were not quite the egalitarians of romantic memory. Instead, they expected a popular hierarchy that would dispense justice where the lords had failed.

In this new England, Ball believed everything would be held in common. This was based on the example of the early church and fair distribution of resources among peasants. It is difficult to be precise about what was envisaged but we get an indication in an account of the meeting of Tyler and Richard II where rebel demands included the waters, parks, and woods being made common to all so that they could hunt without restraint.

There are indications of some sort of shared class awareness in the uprising. Ball and the rebels re-employed stories about the eucharist, the exodus from Egypt, and Christian salvation to focus on liberation of the producers. The discussion of the generic name 'John Miller' in the letters attributed to Ball highlights those who make the bread for the eucharist. Some degree of class unity is echoed in Ball's famous saying about Adam digging and Eve spinning – their everyday labour is the focal point for the rebels.

Despite Ball's justification for the uprising being grounded in theology and the Bible, this was an interpretation that foregrounded human agency as necessary to implement the divine plan. Ball was said to have proclaimed that God had indicated the time when they could remove the yoke of servitude and rejoice in their long-desired liberty. With reference to the Gospel of Matthew, he then talked about violently overthrowing the power of the lords of the realm and their lackeys in order that England may finally be transformed.

Even if Ball's vision is not the same as ours, it represents a grasping at a better world beyond exploitation. But it was also doomed to fail, and the Bible and theology are hardly a comprehensive guide to what it takes to restructure society. Despite clear levels of organisation and networks, the peasantry and those with related discontents could not form a peasant-led state and overthrow the power of the monarch whom the peasants naively trusted. The base of the uprising remained among small landholders with insufficient connections across the geography of England to control the realm. A.L. Morton, ever attuned to rural life, added another point: the peasant army need to return to farms because 'in June hay time is close at hand.'[2]

Feudalism withers

Yet the uprising clearly indicated that all was not well in English feudal relations. Serfdom was in decline and richer peasants were able to accumulate more wealth thereby further undermining the feudal rental system which, as Rodney Hilton argued, was integral to feudalism.[3] As has been retold many times, England was moving towards new economic relations and towards the transformation to capitalism from within feudal society.

The wars of the fifteenth century, including the Wars of the Roses, helped fatally undermine feudalism in England. The English Reformation then provided a crucial stimulus to the creation of a national identity and a national church which were essential for the development of a bourgeois state. Tensions in the ruling class between traditional Catholic tendencies and reformist ones were present from the beginning of the English Reformation. Nevertheless, they were typically united in fear and loathing of the radical end of the Reformation, particularly that associated with Anabaptism on the continent and memories of the 1381 uprising (indistinguishable in the eyes of some interpreters).

Fears of preachers of 'all things in common' remained, whether real or not. On the English stage, Shakespeare, ensuring his plays met the needs of the censors, could satirise radical religion. Yet at the same time he presented this for a mixed audience, who might have a had different understanding of claims about a transformed world of all things in common, plentiful food and decent drink, as economic crises hit England at the end of the sixteenth century (see, for example, Henry VI, Part II – Act 4.2, 63–67). Around the same time, the anonymous play, *The Life and Death of Jack Straw*, could present the views of the 1381 rebels, if not sympathetically, then straightforwardly (and unusually) without explicit authorial value judgment.

All these tensions were, of course, brought out in the open in the English Revolution where puritanism helped promote and justify a hammer blow to feudalism, paving the way for the rapid development of the bourgeois state. The established church would be stuck in a world of compromises between the old aristocratic and feudal order and emerging bourgeois one from which it has never fully advanced to this day. In the long run, Anglicanism took on a ceremonial function akin to the modern monarchy – useful propagandists for colonialism and imperialism, lacking the political power it once had, yet themselves remaining large landowners.

In the most obvious sense, the seventeenth-century revolution 'from below' failed. Even so, following the postwar Marxist historians, we should not see the varied sects (such as Levellers and Diggers) as pure failures. They certainly had their fair share of fantastical millenarian dreams and backward-looking biblical myths as ways of conceptualising change. But intertwined with these were democratising ideas that, in the long run, were not to be suppressed. More immediately, this also included challenges to traditional understandings of religion that would have important consequences. The Bible was seen as a tool not restricted to the established church or authoritative Protestant teachers. The power of the Bible itself was even undermined by emphases such as the 'inner light' and indwelling of Christ. This, and critical thinking about the biblical text, would feed into the Enlightenment where the traditional authority of the Bible would be challenged as never before.

Capitalism and antagonisms

Understanding of the what the Bible 'really means' shifted accordingly as England and later Britain developed into a bourgeois state. Throughout the eighteenth century, dominant assumptions now involved the Bible authorising bourgeois capitalism, whiggish thought, rule of law, and British superiority.[4] Antagonistic understandings of the Bible and religion from below are less easy to detect but they too were developing. Following the American and French Revolutions, these ideas exploded in English radicalism. After four hundred years of vilification, the ideas associated with Ball and the English uprising were now being discussed positively as examples of how the English had challenged ideas of political exclusion before and could do so again.[5]

Such ideas could still be backward looking in the sense that they wanted a return to a time in Saxon England or some biblical era where there were greater democratic and constitutional freedoms. While they were also forward looking, they sometimes remained utopian, fantastical, apocalyptic, and millenarian.[6] Yet amidst these understandings of Christianity, something else was happening that further foregrounded human agency. Among the most significant, at least in terms of the advancement of European scholarship, was the reconstruction of the figure of Jesus. The traditional image of Jesus as the monarchical, divine ruler of the old feudal order was being challenged by the idea of writing a life of the historical figure of Jesus. By 'historical Jesus' or similar terms, I mean presentations of Jesus as understood in his historical context and reconstructed from behind the Gospel texts, typically shorn of stories about miracles and anything supernatural.

This Jesus was understood as a great moral teacher and exemplar of a great national figure of his day.[7] This phenomenon is often seen as a Germanic bourgeois development (and not without reason). But Britain brought its own significant contribution too. Certainly, the English and wider British intellectual establishment dismissed or overlooked Germanic historical Jesus scholarship, not least because its own authority among the bourgeois elite had been settled historically earlier in Britain. Certainly, religious nonconformity could hinder as well as support the advancement of radicalism and working-class interests. But from below there were new antagonisms of a humanistic bent that challenged bourgeois lives of Jesus.

The most prominent radical interpreter was Thomas Paine in *The Age of Reason* (1794–95) where he argued that practically all we can know of the historical Jesus was that he preached human equality, opposed priestly corruption, and pushed for the liberation of the Jewish people from Roman rule. After Jesus was crucified for sedition, non-Jewish Christians created a mythological system in his name and transformed Jesus into a deity.

Paine's reading was influential in English radicalism and was taken up in Chartism. The Chartist press contains discussion of, and adverts for, the works of Paine on religion alongside Germanic Jesus scholarship. There is also plenty of applied discussion of the historical Jesus. While it is not difficult to find conventional piety in the Chartist press, there are numerous portraits of Jesus without reference to the miraculous or the supernatural. The portrayals are consistent in that they present Jesus effectively as the first Chartist. He was from a labouring or poor background who preached virtue, egalitarianism, discipline, and neighbourliness. He was critical of exploitation, tyranny, the rich, religious authorities, and the middle and upper classes of his day. The only significant difference that emerges within the Chartist press is whether this Jesus was prepared to use violence, paralleling some of the debates about moral and physical force in Chartism itself.[8]

Chartists turned to Ball and Tyler in similar ways, not least because this tradition was easily interpreted in terms of class relations. These emphases on Jesus, the English uprising, and class confrontation should therefore be seen as part of the movement towards a class consciousness in the nineteenth century. Related to this is what we see in English Chartism (at least), namely a de-mystifying of the radical religious heritage, even if sometimes unintentionally, and rethinking the stories of the past into near-timeless categories of class distinction applicable across time and place. Part of the explanation of this de-mystifying of Jesus is that beliefs about backward-looking myths and expectations of divine intervention were coming up against the potential power of mass movements to bring about change in the present and future. Jesus had to be rewritten accordingly.

The future

The quest for the historical Jesus would soon be domesticated in the second half of the nineteenth century as the Anglican and intellectual establishment embraced developments in Germanic theology. But the story of religion and radicalism continued with the rise of British socialism. Perhaps the most influential example is William Morris. In *A Dream of John Ball* (1888), Morris creatively reapplied and transformed the apocalypticism of both Ball and Jesus into a historical materialist framework. In this story, Morris (here as the character The Man from Essex) effectively makes himself the secularised seer of the future as he explains to Ball in such religious-inspired language the transformation from feudalism to capitalism and the expectation of the transformation to socialism (and later, as Morris explained elsewhere, to communism). Morris's understanding of the promise of medieval England and its religion, where workers were not alienated from the product of their labour as they would be under capitalism, would be fulfilled under socialism.

Morris had a profound influence on socialist understandings of religion, at least in England. The women's suffrage movement referred back to Morris's form of medievalism and figures such as Ball before a tradition of women's radicalism was developed.[9] British socialism and then communism (including the British Marxist historians) fused Morris's ideas with those of Marx, Engels, and Soviet thinkers to produce a more scientific understanding of religion in terms of human societal evolution, its historic role in class exploitation, its uses in challenging exploitation in pre-capitalist societies, and its absorption into socialist and communist thinking.[10] The pageants of the 1930s included Ball and references to Christian radicalism as well as Morris, Harry Pollitt, and Felecia Browne, the communist who died fighting in Spain.[11] Some of the overlaps between communism and Christianity even led to a CPGB attempt at a dialogue between the two traditions.[12]

But the promises of religion have been absorbed in British socialism to the extent that religion is almost forgotten, and not without reason. Religion has not disappeared from Britain. Its historic authority is still invoked by politicians and the ruling class, as well as in challenges to ruling-class hegemony (for example, by Jeremy Corbyn). But today politicians are generally very wary, and the public typically do not trust politicians invoking religion. In England (and probably Wales and Scotland too), the power of Christianity to rouse class interests (from above or below) is, historically speaking, severely diminished.[13] That the far right has tried and failed to recruit through promoting Christianity against Islam and Muslims is partly a testimony to this weakness.

Conclusion

Christianity has an integral place in retelling the story of English and wider British radical history – as does its demise. One of the advances of the postwar British Marxist historians was to understand millenarianism and apocalypticism as a product of pre-capitalist vehicles of discontent. Yet, what they also showed was how such beliefs were absorbed into resistance to capitalism in socialist and communist movements and parties. Such a thesis is debated to this day, but I would contend in England, at least, this is precisely what has happened. Religion lacks the power to produce, let alone sustain, serious resistance to capitalism. Yet, religious-flavoured resistance and language remains in English culture and religious socialists and communists are found side-by-side (if occasionally uneasily) with non-religious comrades. That this happens is also a testimony to the argument of the British Marxist historians, namely that the yearning for societal transformation in socialism and in communist thinking is the absorption and secularised development of older religious beliefs. Morris might equally have been writing about the fate of religion in Chapter Four of *A Dream of John Ball* when The Man from Essex famously reflected on lost battles and how 'the thing that they fought for comes about in spite of their defeat, and when it comes turns out not to be what they meant, and other men have to fight for what they meant under another name'.

Notes

1   A full discussion of the 1381 revolt, including sources summarised here and bibliography, is available in J. Crossley, *Spectres of John Ball: The Peasants' Revolt in English Political History* (Equinox, Sheffield: 2022), 3–45.

2   A.L. Morton, *When the People Arose: The Peasants' Revolt of 1381* (Communist Party of Great Britain, London: 1981), 29.

3   R. Hilton, *Bond Men Made Free: Medieval Peasant Movements and the English Rising of 1381* (Routledge, London: 1973).

4   See, Y. Sherwood, 'Bush's Bible as a Liberal Bible (Strange though that Might Seem)', *Postscripts*, 2 (2006): 47–58; R. Boer and C. Petterson, *Idols of Nations: Biblical Myth at the Origins of Capitalism* (Fortress Press, Minneapolis: 2014).

5   See, J. Thelwall, *The Peripatetic* (London, 1793), 23–28; J. Baxter, *A New and Impartial History of England* (London, 1796); Robert Southey, *Wat Tyler* (London, 1817).

6   See, T. Evans, *Christian Policy, the Salvation of the Empire* (London, 1816).

7   H. Moxnes, *Jesus and the Rise of Nationalism: A New Quest for the Nineteenth Century Historical Jesus* (I.B. Tauris, London: 2011).

8   For a summary, see J. Crossley, 'The Historical Jesus and Marxist Historiography', *Communist Review* 109 (2023): 16–22.

9   See, *Votes for Women* (8 August 1913); C.P. Collette, '"Faire Emelye": Medievalism and the Moral Courage of Emily Wilding Davison,' *The Chaucer Review* 42 (2008): 223–43 (239–39).

10   A classic statement of this position is A.L. Morton, 'Communism and Morality', in J. Lewis, K. Polanyi, and D. K. Kitchen (eds), *Christianity and the Social Revolution* (London: Gollancz, 1935), 329–355.

11   See, *Daily Worker* (21 Sept. 1936); London District Committee, *The March of English History* (Communist Party of Great Britain, London: 1936).

12   J. Klugmann and P. Oestreicher (eds.), *What Kind of Revolution? A Christian-Communist Dialogue* (Panther Books, London: 1968).

13   J. Crossley, *Cults, Martyrs, and Good Samaritans: Religion in Contemporary English Political Discourse* (Pluto, London: 2018).

10 DAVID HORSLEY

Black communists in Britain: the untold story

W HEN I WAS asked to contribute a chapter to this book, dedicated to the life and work of John Foster, I was first surprised and then very proud to be involved in this tribute to an outstanding communist. Not least as the themes of workplace struggle and community resistance prominent in John's work are those that have inspired my own research journey into the unexplored lives of Black activists.

My contribution showcases the little known but very important part Black women and men played in the history of the Communist Party in Britain, which from the very beginning was both multi-racial and anti-racist. From the early 1920s until the 1960s, Rajani Palme Dutt, of Indian descent, played a prominent role in the leadership and Indian-born Shapurji Saklatvala, as Member of Parliament for Battersea, was probably the most well-known communist in the country during the 1920s. While the focus of this chapter is on communists of African and Caribbean origin or descent, it is important to acknowledge that the contribution of those of Asian heritage was also significant and would repay further research on the conjunction of class and ethnicity.

There is a rich vein of Black communists throughout the history of the British communism, which continues unbroken to this day. Their activism covers all fields: as trade unionists; in anti-colonial and anti-imperialist work; in international solidarity, anti-racism and anti-fascism; working within localities and communities; participating in elections and in the written word. One person who encapsulates all these areas was the starting point for my research, Billy Strachan. Born in 1921 in Jamaica, he travelled at his own expense to Britain at the outbreak of the Second World War, aged eighteen, to enlist in the RAF and rose to the rank of flight lieutenant, flying many missions over Germany and Nazi-occupied Europe. His wartime service made him acutely aware of fascism and racism, and by 1947 he had joined the Communist Party of Great Britain (CPGB) and established the London branch of the anti-colonial and socialist Caribbean Labour Congress. He also started *Caribbean News*, the pioneering anti-colonial, socialist and anti-racist newspaper, and was a leading civil rights pioneer. He later qualified as a barrister, becoming Chief Clerk of Courts and was an active trade unionist. This *precis* of his life does not do him full justice, but first-hand testimony from some of his Caribbean communist comrades is eloquent. Cleston Taylor, a fellow Jamaican who came to Britain and immediately joined the CPGB, told me in a series of oral history interviews 'Billy was the leader of Caribbean communists in the country... [his] flat was used for meetings and became a university of the left for West Indians in the UK... Billy and the Caribbean Labour Congress gave me my real political education.'[1] Trevor Carter stayed with the Strachan family in London when he arrived from Trinidad and, as his wife Corinne Skinner Carter later wrote, 'Billy Strachan was Trevor's mentor'.[2] Winston Pinder, a Barbadian, who arrived in London in 1955, simply told me 'Billy was our father'.[3] A simple tribute that speaks volumes for his influence on a generation of Black communists.

When I researched Billy Strachan's life, I discovered a huge archive at London University. He had also been interviewed on his early life and wartime experiences by the Imperial War Museum. These combined with interviews with the Caribbean communist contemporaries noted above resulted in a booklet published in 2019 by Caribbean Labour Solidarity, with the approval of his eldest son Chris.[4]

My next venture into research produced *The Political Life and Times of Claudia Jones*.[5] I wanted to combat recent works on Jones that, while generally positive, were marred by anti-communism. In short, I wanted to reclaim her for the Communist Party. Over decades, I had located not only a range of secondary material on her life and work, but also amassed papers and journals from the communist movement in the UK and USA.[6] Combining these with oral history interviews, I strove to show that although she was a brilliant communist in her own right, Jones always worked as part of a collective. In the Communist Party of the USA, she had exceptional comrades, Black and white, who helped shape her ideas and theories. In Britain, her major contribution outside the Party was the foundation of the *West Indian Gazette*, where she was surrounded by admiring young Black people who valued her experience and writing very highly and contributed to the paper's success. Her premature death in December 1964, due to health problems exacerbated by harsh imprisonment in the USA and repeated hospitalisations, robbed the Party of perhaps the most outstanding Black communist of all.

This was followed by the compilation of ten brief biographies of Black communists for the collection *Red Lives* in 2020.[7] Those of significant Caribbean activists, such as Trevor Carter and Cleston Taylor, were made easier because I had interviewed them years earlier. Carter arrived in London from Trinidad in 1954 and told me that: 'Joining the YCL [Young Communist League] was a similar experience for me as the feeling of elation Paul Robeson described when he first went to the Soviet Union'. He remained a member of the CPGB until 1991 and died in 2008. Cleston Taylor had been blacklisted for his trade union activity in Jamaica and made a new life for himself in

London in 1952, joining the Party on arrival. He was deeply involved in anti-colonial work and as a skilled carpenter became an activist in the Amalgamated Society of Woodworkers. He told me that he was proud of being elected shop steward on all the building sites where he worked – a great achievement in a mainly white industry. Born in 1926, Taylor, who was also a co-founder of Caribbean Labour Solidarity in the 1970s, died in 2010. There was less information immediately available for Henry Gunter, a Jamaican communist born in 1920, and based in Birmingham, but I later discovered a remarkable record of trade union and anti-racist work. In 1955, for example, the Birmingham branch of the CPGB published his pamphlet *A Man's a Man*, which outlined racism not only in employment and housing in that city, but also in elements of the trade union movement. Gunter died in 2007.

It was particularly rewarding to discover the only Black British International Brigadier, Charlie Hutchison. Born in Oxfordshire in 1918, he joined the YCL aged just seventeen and spent ten years actively fighting fascism, first at Cable Street in October 1936, and two months later in Spain where he joined the International Brigades. He served until the end of 1938, and when Second World War began, he enlisted in the army, seeing service at Dunkirk, in North Africa and Italy, and eventually joining the advance into Germany. There he witnessed the liberation of Belsen in 1945 – the ultimate expression of racist-fascist ideology. A communist until the end of his life, his modesty and humility meant that it was only after his death that his deeds were known.

A chance search of Graham Stevenson's invaluable *Communist Biographies* made me aware of Winifred 'Win' Langton.[8] She was born in 1909 in East London, her mother a foundation member of the Communist Party and her father a militant trade unionist, the son of a freed slave from British Guiana (now Guyana). In 1925, young Win marched with many others to Wandsworth Prison to demand the freedom of leaders of the CPGB, and during the General Strike she cycled round London delivering messages for the strikers. A most active communist through the Hunger Marches and the Second World War, and then campaigning for peace and against apartheid, she joined the women protesting at Greenham Common. Her tireless work for medical aid for Vietnam culminated in the award of a medal and an invitation to visit a Vietnamese hospital that her campaigning had helped build. She died in 2003, her life mirroring the history of British communism in the twentieth century.

I was already aware of the Negro Welfare Association (NWA), which became another important forum for Black activism. The NWA was set up in 1931 by the CPGB after prompting from Black activists in Britain, particularly seamen, and from the Communist International and Profintern – the Red International of Labour Unions (RILU). Unlike the League of Coloured Peoples which has attracted greater attention, the NWA was a militant organisation, fighting colonialism and imperialism throughout the world, while combatting racism and organising in trade unions at home. Its members also supported Black families and organised holidays for working-class Black children. Arnold Ward, a communist seaman based in Britain, was its General Secretary and served as the British representative on the editorial board of the *Negro Worker* journal. Ward, born in Barbados in 1888, was elected to the committee of the League Against Imperialism and led NWA campaigns for justice for the Scottsboro Boys, framed in Alabama for rape and under sentence of death. He was a stalwart of the organisation throughout the 1930s and Hakim Adi records that Paul Robeson credited Ward with at least some of the responsibility for encouraging his first visit to the Soviet Union.[9]

Among other Black communists who worked within the NWA during the 1930s was Harry O'Connell, a seaman from British Guiana, who arrived in Cardiff before First World War, and spent many years organising in the Black community and against racism in the National Union of Seamen. He attended international meetings of the RILU and stood as a CPGB candidate in Cardiff local elections in the 1950s. Desmond Buckle, from the Gold Coast (now Ghana), joined the NWA and went on to become one of the Communist Party's leading experts on African affairs. Born in 1910, he was a member of the Colonial Committee and later the International Committee of the Party, writing articles for the *Daily Worker* and *Labour Monthly*. Buckle wrote *Africa in World History* for the Communist Party History Group in 1959, one of the first Marxist accounts of that continent in English. When he died in 1964, Palme Dutt in an obituary, wrote: 'In the fight for national liberation against Imperialism, Desmond Buckle fulfilled a foremost and honoured role during the thirty years I have known him. He was one of the first African Marxists, a member of the Communist Party and a close friend and associate of African and West Indian fighters'.[10]

Peter Blackman was born in Barbados in 1909 and was also active in the NWA. As a member of the League of Coloured Peoples, he ensured that its journal *Keys* took a more militant outlook in the late 1930s.[11] He had been sent to Britain to be trained as a priest but after travelling to the Gambia in 1935, he was appalled by the racism he witnessed there, and on returning to Britain promptly joining the CPGB. During Second World War, he worked in a factory producing Lancaster bombers, as well as contributing to the Party's *Colonial Information Bulletin*. An outstanding poet, his masterpiece published in 1952 by Lawrence and Wishart was *My Song Is for All Men*, inspired by the ruins of the Warsaw Ghetto, which he had visited with Paul Robeson. Another brilliant work was *Stalingrad*, a tribute to inspirational struggle of the Soviet people against the Nazis.

The city of Liverpool gave the CPGB several significant Black members. One of the most influential was Dorothy Kuya. Born in 1933, she was selling the *Daily Worker* and speaking on street corners as a young teenager. She trained first to be a nurse and then a teacher, and after moving to London joined other communist women in founding the influential journal, *Dragon's Teeth*, which analysed racism in children's books. Returning to her native city, Kuya organised other Liverpudlians fighting the demolition of housing in Black and working-class areas. She successfully campaigned for a slavery museum in her native city, recognising that the slave trade had created Liverpool's wealth. She died in 2013, gaining deserved recognition when students at the city's university by a huge majority voted to rename Gladstone Hall, Dorothy Kuya Hall.[12]

One of Kuya's mentors in Liverpool was Ludwig Hesse, a communist seaman from the Gold Coast, who was instrumental in organising Black citizens battling racism in the 1940s and 1950s. He died in 1987, no longer a communist, but still a Pan-African activist.

Through ex-communists in Liverpool, I also discovered Eric Caddick, born in that city in 1929. He joined the CPGB in the early sixties and as a seaman, worked closely with Jack Coward and other communists in the 1966 seaman's strike, denounced by the then Labour Prime Minister Harold Wilson as being led by 'a tightly knit group of motivated men'. Eric Caddick was also one of the underground anti-apartheid activists who became famous as 'the London Recruits'. Along with other communist seamen, he was approached to join a ship in Mogadishu and take Umkhonto We Sizwe fighters to a designated area on the East African coast. Due to engine breakdown, the fighters had to disembark before their destination with several arrested and jailed. Another Black communist seaman, Gerry Wan, sailed regularly on Union Castle Line ships to Durban. He was entrusted with acting as a courier, carrying messages, documents and money for the African National Congress. Both Caddick and Wan, alongside other Liverpudlians, are now honoured with a plaque at Jack Jones House in Liverpool.

Other notable Black communists featured in my oral history research include Winston Pinder, who after decades as a Party activist became a full-time youth worker in his city.[13] Lionel and Pansy Jeffrey, a couple from British Guiana, played significant roles in the anti-colonial struggle and also went on to do important community work.[14] Len Johnson from Manchester, prevented by racism from being a British boxing champion in the inter-war years, stood as CPGB candidate several times in local elections. Patrick Barrington, also from British Guiana, was an accomplished artist who ran a café-bar with his wife in south London which welcomed those ostracised by society and famously ejected Sarah Ferguson from their premises. Jimmie Barzey from

Montserrat, despite a serious disability, arrived in London aged sixteen in 1953 and became a master tailor. In later years he was a Community Relations Officer.[15]

To conclude, I have attempted to raise the profile of Black communists in Britain. These women and men should be recognised for their contributions to the communist movement from the 1920s onwards. Like many communists, their courage and sacrifice were remarkable, but as well as their day-to-day work as Party activists in a variety of settings, Black communists were also an inspiring presence within the Black community as advisers and support workers. The breadth of their commitment was remarkable, and their story deserves to be told.

Notes

1   Interviews with Cleston Taylor, 1999-2000.
2   Interviews with Trevor Carter, 1999-2000; C.S Carter, *Why Not Me: From Trinidad to Albert Square via Empire Road* (Black Stock Books: 2011).
3   Interview with Winston Pinder, 2019.
4   David Horsley, Billy Strachan, 1921-1998 (Caribbean Labour Solidarity: 2019). Veteran communist, Mike Squires worked with me on the interviews in 1999-2000 for this publication, while Phil Katz also provided post-publication support.
5   D. Horsley, *The Political Life and Times of Claudia Jones* (Manifesto Press, Croydon: 2020). I am grateful to Phil Katz and Tony Conway for entrusting me with this task.
6   B. Johnson *I Think of My Mother: The Life and Times of Claudia Jones* (Karia Press, London: 1985); C. Boyce Davies (Ed.), Claudia Jones: *Beyond Containment: Autobiographical Reflections, Essays and Poems* (Ayebia Clarke, London: 2011).
7   S. Meddick, L. Payne and P. Katz (eds), *Red Lives: Communists and the Struggle for Socialism* (Manifesto Press, Croydon: 2020).
8   G. Stevenson, *Encyclopedia of Communist Biographies.* https://grahamstevenson.me.uk/category/commiepedia/
9   H. Adi, *Pan-Africanism and Communism: The Communist International, Africa and the Diaspora, 1919-1939* (Africa World Press UK, London: 2013).
10 H. Adi, 'Forgotten Comrade? Desmond Buckle: An African Communist in Britain', *Science and Society*, 70, 1 (2006), 22-45.
11 C. Searle, 'Preface', *Footprints: Five Poems* by Peter Blackman (Smokestack Books, Thirsk: 2013).
12 R. Costello, *Liverpool Black Pioneers* (The Bluecoat Press, Liverpool: 2007).
13 Interview with Winston Pinder, 2019.
14 Interview with Pansy Jeffrey, 1999-2000.
15 Interview with Liz Barzey, 2023. Also interviews with Richard Hart (1999-2000), Chris Le Maitre (1999-2000), Jean Tate (2022) and Steve Munby (2023).

Intergenerational psychosocial trauma: violence, social murder and the 'space between'[1]

VIOLENCE IS an omnipresent phenomenon permeating almost all facets of life. As outlined by Johan Galtung, emphasis is frequently placed on its direct aspects, apparently produced through agency and choice, when violence is instead a multifaceted concept extending beyond the individual.[2] Galtung's concept of 'cultural violence' demonstrates how direct or structural violence is justified and normalised through culture itself. Further accentuating this idea, Slavoj Žižek argues that by emphasising the 'subjective' violence, that of the 'objective' nature is ignored.[3] Objective violence is very similar to that of the 'cultural', in that this form of violence allows capitalism to flourish; it is the chronic exploitation of workers, cuts to vital services and constant wars that are engineered for profit and result in the premature deaths of the proletariat for capitalist interests. Entrenched in this approach is also Engels' concept of 'social murder', the notion that systemic violence may in many cases lead to premature death, a fact known to politicians who do nothing to change these conditions, while the public readily accept such deaths as normality.[4] But what is it that allows this violence to become normalised? How is this hegemony shaped? And what of this space between, when violence is not enough to kill but has a lasting detrimental effect on the population it encounters? This essay addresses such questions by exploring dominant hegemonic narratives with reference to Glasgow during the early 2000s. These narratives would play a role in the re-shaping of understandings around class and the emphasis on direct violence, while creating a moral hierarchy of victimhood that disenfranchised the most impoverished. In attending to such phenomena, this essay seeks to provide an introductory insight into violence, social murder and a new theory around 'intergenerational psychosocial trauma', as the 'space between'.

Since the postmodernist turn in academia, the concept of class has become a matter deemed secondary to that of the individual and micro-interactional. Class is no longer viewed as the foundational component in all relations but has been reduced to a mere complication – an 'ism', that can be rectified through language and tokenistic notions of access. The 'class ceiling', for example, with its intrinsic implication that there is something more for the proletariat to aspire to beyond their class, in turn unconsciously legitimising the same system that deceives from behind the guise of meritocracy. Of course, this is simply the latest iteration of class denial, for only two decades have passed since the same postmodernists proclaimed that class was dead. It was the 'end of history', the victory of capitalism, and the abundance of wealth seemingly apparent throughout society would mean that class conflict was no longer a concern for the masses.[5]

However, despite these postmodernist assertions of class obsolescence, the structures of capitalism continue to harm the poorest across society, highlighting the contradictions in any claim regarding the end of class. The reasoning behind these narratives was to obscure the evident systemic violence suffered predominately by the proletariat, but what it also did was reconfigure this notion of the 'underclass.'[6] Where previously the underclass was a grouping which existed below class, in a classless society the existence of an underclass would become an oxymoron. What this meant was a return to Social Darwinist thought, emphasising a natural hierarchy rooted in inborn capabilities fixed by a 'biological inheritance'.[7] Naturally, there was no biological exploration, and instead emphasis was placed only on subjective and socially-ingrained conservative perspectives around behaviours, dress, accents and attitudes. This included even those within the labour market – a particularly important factor given the rise of in-work poverty with the adoption of neoliberalist policies in Glasgow and beyond.[8]

Derogatory and dehumanising terms such as 'Neds' and 'Chavs' became more prominent, and, as suggested by Hayward and Yar, marked the invention of a 'new underclass.'[9] The seemingly sudden emergence of such groups was presented as something more problematic than anything before, creating a new moral panic. However, this was more than panic; these ideas allowed simultaneously for the re-arranging of the lines determining the respectable and non-respectable, those with morals and those without, with definitions of these terms existing as fluid and unfixed, allowing the user to choose their meanings when it suited. Of course, this was not a new practice – the 'dangerous classes', 'problem people', and 'social scum' are all historical examples – but it continued to operate in interests of those who determined the ruling ideas of the epoch.[10] When the figures around poverty and crime – and violence in particular – came to the fore, emphasis was placed on the latter. The new labels allowed for the division of sections within the proletariat. It was not a 'class' issue because class was dead, instead these were 'behavioural issues', born solely of 'agency' – as reflected in policy responses. The result in Scotland was a 'War on Neds', with the 2004 Antisocial Behaviour (Scotland) Act, which created further alienation, social isolation, marginalisation and injustice against what were essentially impoverished populations across the country.[11] These outcomes have always been part of what David Harvey describes as the 'conditions of capitalism', but in this instance, the moral panic on an ideal level, and the Anti-Social Behaviour Order (ASBO) on the material, were instruments to both uphold and recreate these capitalist conditions for an evolving neoliberal society within late capitalism.[12]

Such examples highlighted how violence was to be understood; it was not a product of other forces, but the sole problem that demanded attention. These same narratives have been echoed in recent years by those who take much of the credit for the decline in violence in Scotland since the mid-2000s. The Scottish Violence Reduction Unit (SVRU), for example, founded in 2005 by Strathclyde Police in response to rising homicide rates, suggests that violence is 'a disease' and is contagious, spreading not just across areas but in time too.[13] This 'epidemiological approach' is built along lines of intervention to find out 'who is at risk and stop them catching it'.[14] Such methods have been considered revolutionary, but analysis of this area has neglected the evident paradox in this position. Again, emphasis is placed on the individual who is 'at risk', but while acknowledging that this risk exists, the approach aims only to remove the individual from the conditions, rather than challenging the conditions themselves. This is not an attempt to degrade or belittle the importance of the SVRU, who are constrained by both funding and support, but is intended to highlight the deep-rooted and normalised nature of this systemic harm.

Thus, to challenge violence, one must understand the conditioning and the learned behaviours which play a role in the actions of individuals who commit it, not as an imaginary hand but as a hegemonic regulator for the expressions produced as a consequence of that which is systemic. Carol Craig's attempt at deconstructing Glasgow's history of violence ably detailed the seemingly generational relationship between violence, poverty, and the poor physical and mental health rife amongst the men in the city.[15] Though, beyond attention to alcohol – which is indeed a problem and one again directly linked to systemic harm – it failed to truly grapple with this concept of violence. Nevertheless, there was something deeper that Craig had touched upon, namely that the histories of individuals are not limited to a single period and should be understood as generational and consequential. That is, if one is to understand the behaviours and actions of individuals in the present, there must also be a reflection on that which came before.

Considering Glasgow itself historically, with its excess mortality rates – some of the worst in Western Europe – disproportionate alcohol and drug-death rates, homelessness, and stress-related suicides, these factors are inseparable from the poverty experienced in the lowest strata since the inception of capitalism.[16] Furthermore, in such cases when the result is in fact death, and when the political classes know of such matters but continue with these policies that kill discriminately the poorest and most vulnerable, this becomes Engels' 'social murder'.[17] Therefore, by acknowledging such conditions, one is closer to understanding why the proletariat of specific populations must become 'hardened', not as an individual attribute, but as a collective response across time and place.[18] Against this background, it seems logical to understand that this systemic violence is not simply a contemporary phenomenon but is instead historically grounded, reflecting the imperatives of generational survival and intergenerational resilience in the face of potential social murder.

The term resilience serves as an interesting reminder as to how struggle is generally considered, for inherent in its very being exists a contradiction which normalises the systemic violence that produces a need for it, while simultaneously placing emphasis on the individual who is expected simply to endure such conditions. However, when it is expressed in a manner that does not fit the hegemonic and societal norms dictated by the bourgeoisie, the formerly celebrated notion of resilience is replaced with postmodernist narratives of 'toxic' and 'problematic'.[19] Thus, there is a moral framework infused in these concepts, which shapes not just how to act but how also to respond to one's experiences. In recent years there have been conscious attempts by postmodernist academics to explore such 'lived experiences', but the shortfalls of such approaches are made apparent in these instances, because they too must fall within the remit of 'social acceptability'.[20] In a system where this relationship of violence is promoted as spontaneous and binary, it becomes unlikely that the perpetrator would be considered victim. In fact, these ideological and individualist narratives of the lived experience in many ways work to the detriment of those who are most affected by this systemic harm, particularly when they are consigned to the 'new underclass' and denied a voice. Such issues must be addressed at a systemic level, because only through analysis of the systemic may one bypass these idealist narratives, to fully grasp why such resilience must exist in the first place.

Accordingly, if it is accepted that systemic violence will inflict harm on individuals, and social murder is the term given when such harm is punitive enough to kill, then one must ask: what of the *space between*? With violence in any sense, there is often potential to kill, and for those who survive, there may remain still a consequence – that of trauma. Yet, in regards to this systemic violence, trauma itself is scarcely considered.[21] There have been numerous definitions and diagnostic explanations for trauma across time but generally, trauma can be considered as the lasting emotional response that often results from living through a distressing event.[22] Of course, trauma in the West, like violence, is considered entirely as an individual experience, with definitions rooted in this western and ethnocentric framework. Furthermore, the power to diagnose or determine trauma remains as a power held specifically by those of the middle and upper classes. Therefore, it is only to be expected that the same system benefits those classes who are relatively untouched by the actual experience of trauma.

Nevertheless, when one considers this notion of the 'traumatic event', what then exists when this trauma is not a singular event, but one's entire reality? Is this systemic harm which may lead to social murder not distressing? Is living in this poverty which kills and maims friends and loved ones not traumatic? As noted by Fisher, society is so inculcated with 'capitalist realism' – that there is no other alternative to what exists now – that the arguments made here will be considered radical or even outlandish, because these traumas are presented as normality.[23] However, such examples are normality only for the poor, and so logically the response is amplified in the case of these populations. Born into an environment of harm, surrounded by poverty, illness and death, where the youth are disenfranchised and alienated, and socialised through this harsh systemic violence, and still we ask why these 'toxic behaviours' such as violence are expressed not only in the moment, but also across time and place? Is it mere coincidence that members of this 'new underclass' articulate their trauma as a form of resilience in a manner that rejects the prevailing 'social acceptability', when this same society dubs such individuals good-for-nothing, 'social scum' and worthless? Finally, we must ask then, of what benefit is the lived experience for those who do not exist?

Violence in this context must therefore be understood as an articulation of the trauma bound by the material reality through which the 'new underclass' are born and live their lives. Their very existence, rejected through a denial of class, and their voice considered lesser as they become perpetrators, unconsciously reproduces the same conditions in which they are socialised. Meanwhile, these conditions which breed a requirement for resilience are considered unimportant, because this response does not fit the socially ingrained, conservative ideal of social acceptability. Therefore, when considering that which exists between the systemic violence and social murder, it must also be considered across time and place. This *space between* must be understood as reflecting the generational poverty, and the intergenerational relationship with class, capital and systemic harm, as it produces and reproduces the conditions for the 'new underclass' to exist in. Thus, if we are to challenge such 'toxicity', then violence must be understood and challenged as an expression of *intergenerational psychosocial trauma*, as both a symptom of – and locally based resilience against – this destructive capitalist system. Let not us remain ignorant to the cause when a flower fails to bloom in polluted soil!

Notes

1   I met John Foster around eight years ago in Govan, just as I started to become active in organising in the local area. Since our first encounter, John has been extremely supportive in numerous ways, from putting his faith in me to lead the Govan Communist Party branch, and supporting some of my campaigns, to encouraging and helping me where necessary with my studies. However, it is not what he has done for me which I find most admirable, but in his deeds and his dedication to the struggle. Through times of hardship and despair, he has remained true to the proletariat, and as a communist, I believe there to be no greater honour.

2   J. Galtung, 'Violence, Peace, and Peace Research', *Journal of Peace Research*, 6, 3 (1969), 167-191.

3   S. Žižek, *Violence: Six Sideways Reflections* (Picador, New York: 2008), 8.

4   F. Engels, *Condition of the Working Class in England* (Institute of Marxism-Leninism: Moscow, 1969), 25. Systemic violence is used in this essay intentionally because the issues addressed are not a consequence of a structure that can be tweaked with policies, but instead require full systemic change with an end of capitalism.

5   F. Fukuyama, *The End of History and the Last Man* (Free Press, New York: 1992).

6   B. Jordan and M. Redley, 'Polarisation, Underclass and the Welfare State', *Work, Employment and Society*, 2 (1994), 153–176.

7   C. Collins, P.E. Jones and M. McCrory, 'Transforming theory for a transforming world', *Theory & Struggle*, 121 (2020), 58-67.

8   M. Boyle, C. McWilliams, and G. Rice, 'The Spatialtities of Actually Existing Neoliberalism in Glasgow, 1977 to the Present', *Geografiska Annaler: Series B, Human Geography*, 90, 4 (2008), 313–25.

9   K. Hayward and M. Yar, 'The "Chav" phenomenon: Consumption, media and the construction of a new underclass', *Crime, Media, Culture*, 2 (2006), 9-28. 'Neds' is the favoured colloquial term in the West of Scotland.

10 L. Morris, *Dangerous Classes: The Underclass and Social Citizenship* (Routledge, London: 1994).

11 A. Brown, 'The War on 'Neds': media reports as evidence base, *Criminal Justice Matters*, 59, 1, (2005), 16-17.

12 D. Harvey, *The Condition of Postmodernity: An Enquiry into the Origins of Cultural Change* (Blackwell, Oxford: 1989).

13 Formerly known simply as the Violence Reduction Unit.

14 E. Williams and P. Squires, *A Joined-Up Approach to Sustainable Violence Prevention* (Palgrave, London: 2021).

15 C. Craig, *The Tears that Made the Clyde: Well-Being in Glasgow* (Argyll Publishing, Glendaruel: 2010).

16 G. McCartney et al., 'Has Scotland always been the "sick man" of Europe? An observational study from 1855 to 2006', *The European Journal of Public Health* (2011), 756-60.

17 Engels, *Condition of the Working Class*, 25.

18 S. Damer, *From Moorepark to 'Wine Alley': The Rise and Fall of a Glasgow Housing Scheme* (Edinburgh, UniversityPress, Edinburgh: 1989).

19 See, for example, C. Holligan and R. McLean, 'Violence as an Environmentally Warranted Norm amongst Working-Class Teenage Boys in Glasgow', *Social Sciences*, 7 (2018), 207.

20 For 'social acceptability' see, G. Brewis, 'Driven by Ideology or "Half-Mad" from War? An Investigtion into the Motivations of the Auxiliaries during the Irish War of Independence ', MSc Thesis, (University of Strathclyde, 2021), 26- 30.

21 C. Scanlon and J. Adlam, *Psycho-social Explorations of Trauma, Exclusion and Violence: Un-housed Minds and Inhospitable Environments* (Routledge, London: 2022).

22 A.J. Marsella, 'Ethnocultural Aspects of PTSD: An Overview of Concepts, Issues, and Treatments', Traumatology, 16, 4 (2010), 17-26.

23 M. Fisher, *Capitalist Realism: Is There No Alternative?* (O Books, Winchester: 2009).

Bibliography of Professor John Foster's published work

Monographs

Class Struggle and the Industrial Revolution: Early Industrial Capitalism in Three English Towns (Weidenfeld and Nicolson, London: 1974); (reprinted as a Methuen University Paperback, London: 1977).

(With C. Woolfson), *The Politics of the UCS Work-in: Class Alliances and the Right to Work* (Lawrence & Wishart, London: 1986).

(With C. Woolfson), *Track Record: The Story of the Caterpillar Occupation* (Verso, London: 1988).

[As Convener of the Scottish Trades Union Working Party], *Scotland's Economy: Claiming the Future* (Scottish Trades Union Congress, Glasgow: 1988); (reprinted by Verso, London: 1990).

(With C. Woolfson), *Trade Unionism and Health and Safety in the British Offshore Industry* (International Committee for Trade Union Rights, Dublin: 1992).

(With C. Woolfson and M. Beck), *Paying for the Piper: Capital and Labour in Britain's Offshore Industry* (Mansell, London: 1996).

(With M. Beck, H. Ryggvik and C. Woolfson), *Piper Alpha: Ten Years After* (Centre for Technology and Culture: University of Oslo, Oslo: 1996).

[As Convener of a report commissioned by the Scottish Trades Union Congress and Scottish CND], *Cancelling Trident: the economic and social consequences for Scotland* (Scottish Trades Union Congress and Scottish CND, Glasgow: 2007).

(With M. Davis), *UNITE History Volume 1 (1880-1931): The Transport and General Workers' Union (TGWU): Representing a Mass Trade Union Movement* (Liverpool University Press, Liverpool: 2022).

UNITE History Volume 4 (1960-1974): The Transport and General Workers' Union (TGWU): The Great Tradition of Independent Working Class Power (Liverpool University Press, Liverpool: 2023).

Languages of Class Struggle: Communication and Mass Mobilisation in Britain and Ireland 1842-1972 (Praxis Press, Glasgow: 2024).

Journal Articles

'Revolutionaries in Oldham', *Marxism Today* (November 1968), 335-43.

'How Oldham's Working-Class Leaders Managed to Avoid Reformism, 1812-1847', *Bulletin of the Society for the Study of Labour History*, 16 (1968), 6-10.

'The Making of the First Six Factory Acts', *Bulletin of the Society for the Study of Labour History*, 18 (1969), 5-7.

'The National Question and the British Working-Class Movement', *World Marxist Review*, 10 (1972), 134-138.

'Capitalism and the Scottish Nation', *Scottish Marxist*, 4 (June 1973), 7-16.

'Some Comments on Class Struggle and the Labour Aristocracy, 1830-60', *Social History*, 1 (1976), 357-366.

'The State and the Ruling Class in the 1926 General Strike', *Marxism Today* (May 1976), 137-147.

'Northern Ireland', *Modern Studies Yearbook* (1982), 47-52.

(With G. Kerevan), 'Debate: Scottish Capitalism', *Scottish Marxist* (Spring 1983), 5-7.

'The Merits of the Social Democratic Federation', Marx Memorial Lecture 1984, *Bulletin of The Marx Memorial Library*, 105 (1984), 25-37.

'Moving the Goalposts', *Marxism Today* (March 1985), 43-4.

'British Policies in Northern Ireland since 1979', *Modern Studies Association* (1986), 70-75.

'Scottish Voices', *Scottish Trade Union Review*, 36 [Commemoration Issue for the 70th Anniversary of the Soviet Revolution], (Autumn 1987), 9-11.

'Thatcherism: Trojan horse for the new revisionism', *Communist Campaign Review*, 3 (Spring 1987), 3-8.

'Scotland and the Russian Revolution', *Scottish Labour History Journal*, 23 (1988), 3-14.

(With C. Woolfson), 'Corporate Reconstructionism and Business Unionism: The Lessons of Caterpillar and Ford', *New Left Review*, 174 (March/April 1989), 51-66.

'Strike Action and Working-Class Politics on Clydeside 1914-1919', *International Review of Social History*, 35, 1 (1990), 33-70.

'The Common Market and the National Question in Britain', *Communist Review*, 9 (Spring 1991), 4-13, 27-8.

'Has Communism a Future?', *Modern Studies Yearbook* (1991/92), 56-52.

(With H. Maguiness and A. Munro), 'Scotland's Oil and Gas contracting Industry and the Petroleum Revenue Tax', *Quarterly Economic Commentary* (Fraser of Allander Institute), 14, 4 (1993) 76-83.

'The Case for Communism', *Communist Review*, 35 (Autumn 2001), 18-22.

(With M. Houston and C. Madigan), 'Distinguishing Catholics and Protestants among Irish Immigrants to Clydeside: A New Approach to Immigration and Ethnicity in Victorian Britain', *Irish Studies Review*, 10, 2 (2002), 171-92.

'Oil and American Imperialism', *Communist Review*, 38 (Spring 2003), 8-11.

'Communist Renewal in Scotland 1986-1990', *Scottish Labour History Journal*, 38 (2003), 75-93.

'Marxists, Weberians and Nationality: A Response to Neil Davidson', *Historical Materialism*, 12, 1 (2004), 155-179.

(With S. Baird and R. Leonard), 'Ownership of Companies in Scotland', *Quarterly Economic Commentary* (Fraser of Allander Institute), 29, 3 (2004), 45-53.

(With M. Davis), 'Why were they so afraid of Communist Influence? *American Communist History*, 4, 2 (2005) 167-173.

'Burgerliche Demokratie in Grossbritanien', *Topos: Internationale Beitrage zur Dialectischen Theorie*, Instituto Italiano per gli Studi Filosofici, 24 (2005), 33-58.

(With S. Baird and R. Leonard), 'Scottish Capital: Still in Control in 21st Century Scotland?', *Scottish Affairs*, 58 (Winter 2007), 1-35.

'Connolly on Nationality and Religion: Class Politics and the Second International', *Communist Review*, 48 (Spring 2007), 33-5.

'Cold Death by Neoliberalism: The Political Economy of Fuel Poverty', *Variant*, 28 (Spring 2007), 6-7.

'Trade Unions under Socialism: Perestroika Revisited', *Communist Review*, 49 (Winter 2007/8), 14-18.

(With S. Nisbet), 'Protection, inward investment and the early Irish cotton industry: the experience of William and John Orr', *Irish Economic and Social History*, 35 (2008), 441-67.

'Super-profit, the Super-rich and the Failure of Britain's Ruling Class', *Communist Review*, 56 (Spring, 2010), 8-16.

'The Aristocracy of Labour and Working-Class Consciousness Revisited', *Labour History Review*, 75, 3 (2010), 245-262.

'Irish Immigrants in Scotland's Shipyards and Coalfields: Employment Relations, Sectarianism and Class Formation', *Historical Research* 84, 226 (2011), 657-92.

'Marx, Marxism and the British Working-Class Movement: Some Continuing Issues in the 21st Century', *World Review of Political Economy*, 2, 4 (2011), 671-86.

'The EU Single Market and Employment Rights: from a Dysfunctional to an Abusive Relationship', *Communist Review*, 64 (Summer 2012), 2-7.

(With M. Davis), 'Eric Hobsbawm: Foremost Historian in the Marxist Tradition', *Communist Review*, 66 (Winter 2012/13), 28-9.

'Eric Hobsbawm: A Marxist who Transformed the Writing of History', *Labour History Review*, 78, 3 (2013), 351-71.

'Eric Hobsbawm, Marxism and *Social History*', *Social History*, 39, 2 (2014), 160-171.

'British Overseas Territories: where British and US Imperialism Meet', *Communist Review*, 71 (Spring 2014), 23-7.

'Willie Gallacher – in Praise of an Agitator', *Scottish Labour History Journal*, 50 (2015), 116-123.

'On Marx's Method and the Study of History', *Theory & Struggle*, 116 (2015), 52-59.

'Classes, Nations and Marxism', *Theory & Struggle*, 117 (2016), 121-8.

'Upper Clyde Shipbuilders 1971–2 and Edward Heath's U-turn: How a united workforce defeated a divided government', The Mariner's Mirror, 102, 1 (2016), 34-48.

'The Russian Revolution and the Emergence of the Communist Party in Scotland', *Scottish Labour History Journal*, 52 (2017), 41-53.

'Karl Marx 2018', *Theory & Struggle*, 118 (2018), 133-6.

'Ο Μαρξ και η βρετανικη εργατικη τάξη', Νέος Δημοκράτης,, 119 (December 2018), 19-30.

'Marx and the British Working Class', *Theory & Struggle*, 120 (2019), 2-9.

(With K. MacAskill and R. Scothorne), 'Jimmy Reid Biography Symposium: Reflections on a Changing Communist Clyde-built Man', *Scottish Labour History Journal*, 54 (2019), 58-78.

'The 1919 Forty Hours Strike', *Theory & Struggle*, 121 (2020), 30-41.

(With M. Davis and R. Seifert), 'Three Communist Educators: Robin Page Arnot, James Klugmann and Andrew Rothstein', *Theory & Struggle*, 121 (2020), 108-125.

(With L. Payne, K. Coyle and R. Griffiths), 'Communist Internationalism: Completing the Century', *Communist Review*, 97 (Autumn 2020), 14-22.

(With P. Bryan, J. Driscoll, K. Clark, S. Griffin, A. Murray, K. Neilson and B. Winter), 'The National Question and Progressive Federalism', *Theory & Struggle*, 123 (2022), 46-71.

'The Coming Cuts to Public Spending', *ROSE: Radical Options for Scotland and Europe*, 1 (2024), 5-7.

'State Power, Working-Class Mobilisation and Two Types of Alliance', *Communist Review*, 112 (July-August 2024), 10-16

Chapters and Contributions

'Nineteenth Century Towns – a Class Dimension', in H. J. Dyos (ed.) *The Study of Urban History* (Leicester University Press, Leicester: 1967), 281-99; reprinted M.W. Flynn and T.C. Smout (eds), *Essays in Social History* (Clarendon Press, Oxford: 1972), 176-98.

'The National Question and the British Working Class' [in Russian], in K. Zaradov (ed.), *The Soviet Union in the Contemporary World* (Peace and Socialism, Prague: 1972), 232-236.

'Capitalism and the Scottish Nation', in G. Brown (ed.), *The Red Paper on Scotland* (Edinburgh University Students' Publication Board, Edinburgh: 1975), 141-152.

'British Imperialism and the Labour Aristocracy', in J. Skelley (ed.), *The General Strike 1926* (Lawrence & Wishart, London: 1976), 3-57.

'Urban Studies: some comments on the relationship between the state and the locality', *The Production of the Built Environment, Proceedings of Bartlett Summer School*, 1979 (University College London, London: 1980), 131-5.

'Introduction', in M. Jenkins (ed.), *The General Strike of 1842* (Lawrence & Wishart, London: 1980), 13-19.

'Scottish Capitalism and the Origins of Nationality', in T. Dickson (ed.), *Scottish Capitalism: Class, State and Nation from before the Union to the Present* (John Donald, Edinburgh: 1982), 19-62.

Entries on 'Bourgeoisie' and 'Class', in J. Eatwell, M. Milgrave, P. Newman (eds), *New Palgrave Dictionary of Economics* (Macmillan, London: 1987); reprinted in J. Eatwell, M. Milgrave, P. Newman (eds), *Marxian Economics*, Macmillan, London: 1990), 59-65, 79-85.

'Nationality, Social Change and Class: Class Transformation of National Identity in Scotland', in D. McCrone, S. Kendrick and P. Straw (eds), *The Making of Scotland, Nation, Culture and Social Change* (Edinburgh University Press, Edinburgh: 1989), 31-52; reprinted in Afers: fulls de recerca i pensament, Volume IV (1989), 357-378.

'La Cuidad al Mon Industrial', in, *Colloqui International de Historia Local* (Diputacio de Valencia, Valencia: 1989), 135-57.

'Red Clyde, Red Scotland', in I. Donnachie and C. Whatley (eds), *The Manufacture of Scottish History* (Polygon, Edinburgh: 1992), 106-42.

'A Proletarian Nation? Occupation and Class since 1914', in T. Dickson and J.H. Treble (eds), *People and Society in Scotland, Volume III, 1914-1990* (John Donald, Edinburgh, 1992), 201-40.

'Labour, Keynesianism and the Welfare State', in J. Fyrth (ed), *Labour's High Noon: 1945-1951* (Lawrence & Wishart, London: 1993), 20-36.

'La formation syndicale et le cooperation avec les universitaires en Ecosse', in G. Valenduc (ed.) *La recherche scientifique et le monde de travail* (Foundation Travail-Universitaire, Brussels: 1993).

'Working Class Mobilisation on the Clyde 1917-1920', in C. Wrigley (ed.), *The Challenge of Labour: Central and Western Europe* (Routledge, London: 1993), 149-75.

'The end of history and Historical Materialism: A defence of Marxist dialectics', in M. Davis and M. Mayo (eds), *Marxism and Struggle. Toward the Millennium* (Praxis Press, London: 1998), 29-54.

'Class', in A. Cooke, I. Donnachie, A. MacSween and C. Whatley (eds), Modern Scottish History. *The Modernisation of Scotland: 1850 to the Present* (Tuckwell/Open University, East, 1998), 210-234.

(With C. Woolfson), 'How Workers on the Clyde Gained the Capacity for Class Struggle: The

Upper Clyde Shipbuilders' Work-in, 1971-2', in J. McIlroy, N. Fishman and A. B. Campbell (eds), *The High Tide of British Trade Unionism: Trade Unions and Industrial Politics 1964-79* (Ashgate, Aldershot: 1999); (reprinted Merlin Press: 2007), 297-325.

'Willie Gallacher: A Paisley Communist in Parliament', in, *Essays in the Labour History of Renfrewshire* (Renfrewshire Council/STUC, Paisley: 1999), 25-34.

'The Twentieth Century, 1914-1979', in R.A. Houston and W.W.J. Knox (eds), *The New Penguin History of Scotland: from the Earliest Times to the Present Day* (Allen Lane in association with the National Museums of Scotland, London: 2001), 417-96.

'The Economic Restructuring of the West of Scotland 1945-2000', in G. Blazyca (ed.), *Restructuring of Regional Economies: Towards a Comparative Study of Scotland and Upper Silesia* (Ashgate Press, Aldershot: 2003), 57-69.

'Prologue: What Kind of Crisis? What Kind of Ruling Class?', in A. Campbell, K. Guildart and J. McIlroy (eds), *Industrial Politics and the 1926 Mining Lockout* (University of Wales Press, Cardiff, 2004) 16-43.

'Scotland's Energy Crisis', in V. Mills (ed.), *The Red Paper on Scotland* (Research Collections @ Glasgow Caledonian University, Glasgow: 2005), 37-54.

(With S. Baird and R. Leonard), 'Ownership and Control in the Scottish Economy', in V. Mills (ed.), *The Red Paper in Scotland* (Research Collections @ Glasgow Caledonian University, Glasgow: 2005), 83-105.

'William Pearce 1833-1888, Copper-Trousered Philanthropist' in N. Norrie and R. Adams (eds), *Pearce Institute Centenary Book* (The Pearce Institute, Glasgow: 2006), 99-110.

(With M. Houston and C. Madigan), 'Sectarianism, Segregation and Politics in the Later Nineteenth Century', in M.J. Mitchell (ed.), *New Perspectives on the Irish in Scotland* (John Donald, Edinburgh: 2008), 63-96.

'The Financial Crisis in Britain', in R. Griffiths (ed.), *Arise in Unity: The International Crisis and Alternatives from the Left* (People's Democracy Publications, New Delhi: 2011, 106-17).

(With R. Leonard), 'Introduction (Economy)', in P. Bryan and T. Kane (eds), *Class, Nation and Socialism: The Red Paper on Scotland* 2014 (Glasgow Caledonian University Archives, Glasgow: 2013), 10-11.

(With R. Leonard), 'What's Wrong with Scotland's Economy', in P. Bryan and T. Kane (eds), *Class, Nation and Socialism: The Red Paper on Scotland* 2014 (Glasgow Caledonian University Archives, Glasgow: 2014), 12-15.

'Economic Policy, Class Alliances and Political Influence in Scotland', in P. Bryan and T. Kane (eds), *Class, Nation and Socialism: The Red Paper on Scotland* 2014 (Glasgow Caledonian University Archives, Glasgow: 2014), 22-26.

(With R. Leonard), 'Learning from the Rest of the World', in P. Bryan and T. Kane (eds), *Class, Nation and Socialism: The Red Paper on Scotland* 2014 (Glasgow Caledonian University Archives, Glasgow: 2014), 27-35.

'Nation and Class', in P. Bryan and T. Kane (eds), *Class, Nation and Socialism: The Red Paper on Scotland* 2014 (Glasgow Caledonian University Archives, Glasgow: 2014), 126-132.

'The Scottish Effect: some comments from a historical perspective', in C. Collins, M. Mackenzie and G. McCartney (eds), *Accounting for Scotland's Excess Mortality: Towards a Synthesis. Commentaries and Responses* (Glasgow Centre for Population Health, Glasgow: 2014), 2-8.

(With E. Gibbs, and R. Leonard), 'Federalism, the Scottish Economy and Economic Democracy', in *Progressive Federalism* (Red Paper Collective, Glasgow: 2016), 8-11.

'History and Marx's Method', in M. Davis (ed.), *Marx 200: The Significance of Marxism in the 21st Century* (Praxis Press, London: 2019), 30-39.

'Vote Communist', in M. Davis (ed.), *A Centenary for Socialism. Britain's Communist Party, 1920-2020* (Manifesto Press, Croydon: 2020), 78-91.

'The Communist Party and the 1926 General Strike', in M. Davis (ed.), *A Centenary for Socialism: Britain's Communist Party, 1920-2020* (Manifesto Press, Croydon: 2020), 117-125.

'Working for Class Unity in Extreme Circumstances', in M. Davis, *UNITE History Volume 5 (1974-1992) From Zenith to Nadir?* (Liverpool University Press: Liverpool: 2023), 105-120.

'Where Solidarity Defeated Thatcherism', in M. Davis, *UNITE History Volume 5 (1974-1992): From Zenith to Nadir?* (Liverpool University Press, Liverpool: 2023), 121-134.

Review Essays

'The Risings of the Luddites, Chartists and Plug Drawers' [F. Neal], *Bulletin of the Society for the Study of Labour History*, 21 (1970), 29-32.

'How Imperial London Preserved its Slums' [A. Wohl], *International Journal of Urban and Regional Research*, 3 (1979), 93-114.

'Karl Marx's Theory of History: A Defence' [G.A. Cohen], *Marxism Today* (October 1981), 43-47.

'The Declassing of Language' [G. Stedman-Jones], *New Left Review*, 1/150 (March/April 1985), 29-45.

'A New History of Scotland' [C. Harvie], *Journal of Scottish Social and Economic History*, 6, 1 (1986), 65–68.

'Conflict at Work' [P.K. Edwards], *Social History*, 14, 2 (1989), 233-41.

'Can Workers Have a Voice' [D.A. Hathaway], *Labour History Review*, 60, 1 (1995), 128-9.

'The Origins of Scottish Nationhood' [N. Davidson], *Historical Materialism*, 10, 1 (2002), 258-71.

'Raising Questions which Socialists Need to Answer: Review of *The New Stage of Capitalism*' [Z. Tongyu et al.], *Communist Review*, 66 (Winter 2012/13), 32-3.

'British Twentieth Century History', *Theory & Struggle*, 116 (2015), 70-3.

'Valuable Resource for Political Education and Debate: *Marx 200: a Review of Marx's Economics 200 Years After his Birth*' [M. Roberts], *Communist Review*, 99 (Autumn 2019), 30-31.

Pamphlets

'The development of positive multi-cultural relations: a local initiative in Scotland', in *Reflections* (Bangladesh Association of Scotland, 1986).

Scotland and Socialism (CPB Scotland, Glasgow: 1993).

Scotland and Democracy (CPB Scotland, Glasgow: 1994).

Scotland and its Economy (CPB Scotland, Glasgow: 1994).

Scotland, Europe and the World (CPB Scotland, Glasgow: 1996).

Talking about Socialism [John Foster in discussion with Tony Benn] (Unity Books, Glasgow: 1996).

A Plan for Scotland's Economy (CPB Scotland, Glasgow: 2000).

(With R. Leonard), 'Star wars , the Scottish economy and the economics of dependency, in, *Star Wars. Space – the Next Target for US Invasion* (Scottish Campaign for Nuclear Disarmament, Glasgow: 2004).

Breaking the British State. The way forward to socialism in Scotland (CPB Scotland, Glasgow: 2004).

The Communist Party and the Labour Movement: Elections and Class Struggle (Communist Party of Britain, London: 2007).

Economics for Workers (Communist Party of Ireland, Dublin: 2009).

The Politics of Britain's Economic Crisis (Communist Party of Britain, Croydon: 2009).

Africa and British Imperialism Today (Communist Party of Britain, Croydon: 2009).

The European Union: For the Monopolies, Against the People (Communist Party of Britain, Croydon: 2011).

(With R. Griffiths), *Which Road for China? Report on the 2011 Delegation of European Communist Parties* (Communist Party of Britain, Croydon: 2011).

The EU and Alternatives to Austerity (Communist Party of Britain, Croydon: 2012).

[Contributor], *Building an Economy for the People* (Manifesto Press, Croydon: 2012).

'Economic Development, Progressive Values and Scotland as a Nation', in P. Bryan (ed.), *People Power: The Labour Movement Alternative for Radical Constitutional Change* (Red Paper Collective, Glasgow: 2012) 13-5.

European Union Withdrawal. The People's Answer to Austerity (Communist Party of Britain, Croydon: 2013).

'The 1971-2 work-in revisited: How Clydeside's workers defeated a Tory government', *Our History* (pamphlet No. 9 - new series) (Communist Party of Britain, Croydon: 2013).

(With A. Mackinnon), 'Why Class Politics?' in Pauline Bryan (ed.), *Scotland: Myths, Realities and Radical Future* (Red Paper Collective, Glasgow: 2015), 15-19.

'Introduction', in *The EU Deconstructed: Critical Voices from Denmark, Portugal, Cyprus and Germany* (Manifesto Press, Croydon: 2016), 1-3.

The Councils of Action 1920 and the British Labour Movement's Defence of Soviet Russia (Manifesto Press, Croydon: 2017).

Johnson's post-EU Britain or progressive federalism (Communist Party of Britain, Croydon: 2021).

Nations and Working-Class Unity in Britain (Communist Party of Britain, Croydon: 2023).

Sources and Other Outputs

John Foster (Poll Tax) Papers [1988-92], The Archive Centre, Glasgow Caledonian University.

Miscellaneous campaign literature produced by John Foster for the General Election of 7 June 2001, MMSID: 9939379643804341, National Library of Scotland.

'Shipbuilding, class consciousness and the Clyde, 1900-1970s', Seminar Series of the Glasgow Labour History Workshop, University of Strathclyde, 16 February 1988.

'Strike Action and Working-Class Politics on Clydeside, 1914-1919', International Colloquium, Graz, 9 June 1989.

Interview with John Foster by Neil Rafeek, 1994-11-23,www.nms.ac.uk, ISRC: CKEY8277524.

'Overcoming Social Exclusion: Comments on current strategies', Paper for the Lord Provost's Commission on Overcoming Social Exclusion in Edinburgh, University of Paisley, 1999.

John Foster interviewed by Alan Campbell and Jon McIlroy, Tape 656, 2000-05-03, Communist Party of Great Britain Biographical Project, British Library Sound Collections (Copy also in the Working Class Movement Library, Salford).

'Britain and the US strategy for world domination: The struggle for popular sovereignty and democracy', Contribution from the Communist Party of Britain, International Conference of Communist and Workers Parties, Lisbon, 10-12 November 2006.

'Resisting the languages of control: A comparison of working-class mobilisation on Clydeside in 1919 and 1971, Colloque Internationale Lyon: Discours et dispositifs anti-syndicaux, Lyon, 5-6 November 2010.

Interview with Professor Emeritus John Foster by Linette Sullivan, 2016-08-20, https://docplayer.net/11488626-Interview-with-emeritus-professor-john-foster-social-sciences-university-of-the-west-of-scotland.html

'The Russian Revolution and the Emergence of the Communist Party in Scotland', Scottish Labour History Society Annual Conference, John Smith House, Glasgow, 4 November 2017, https://www.youtube.com/watch?v=GfijmTzhwtA&ab_channel=CommunistParty

(With T.Conway, R. Griffiths and L. Payne), 'Fascism in Britain: Past and Present' [Letter/Discussion], *Communist Review*, 90 (Winter 2018/9), 2-5.

'Why We Need a Radical Economic Strategy', Red Paper Collective Post, 19 May 2021, https://redpapercollective.net/?p=114

INDEX